WAR STORIES

Accounts of Minnesotans Who Defended Their Nation

By Al Zdon

A PROJECT OF THE MINNESOTA
AMERICAN LEGION

MOONLIT EAGLE PRODUCTIONS
2002

War Stories,
Accounts of Minnesotans Who Defended Their Nation

Copyright 2002, The Minnesota American Legion
All Rights Reserved

Printed in the United States of America by Stanton
Publications, St.Paul

Published by Moonlit Eagle Productions
5064 Irondale Road
Mounds View, MN 55112

First Edition

ISBN 0-9711940-1-7

Moonlit Eagle
Productions

DEDICATION

To my father, Joseph P. "Jeff" Zdon, who served in Europe in World War II, and to my mother, Marie, who served on the homefront.

ACKNOWLEDGMENTS

I started writing accounts of people who served in the wars for the *Minnesota Legionnaire* about six years ago. Eventually, there were enough stories to make a book. The impetus for actually doing it, though, came from the need to raise funds for the World War II Memorial in Minnesota. The sole beneficiary of this book is that memorial.

Along the way there were many who helped. In particular, the World War II History Round Table at the Ft. Snelling History Center, under the direction of Don Patton, provided a wealth of stories for the Legionniare and this book.

There were several Legion leaders who played important roles in getting the book published. Adjutant Lyle Foltz heard the idea first and gave it great support. And, at a meeting in Washington D.C., Department Commander Bill Goede, Past National Commander Dan Ludwig and Past National Commander Dan Foley gave the direction the book needed to move it from the drawing board to the printers. The Minnesota American Legion Foundation and the Department Finance Committee provided the money to print it. Department Commander Don Hayden has continued that strong support during his year at the helm.

Thanks to proofreaders Larissa Zdon and Karla Kruger for finding hundreds of mistakes. Thanks to Louise Lundin for the wonderful cover painting and to Liina Koukkari who did an outstanding job in designing both the interior pages and the cover.

Most of all, the book wouldn't be possible without the willingness of about 30 veterans from different wars to tell their stories candidly and with emotion and humor. Their stories need to be told and need to be preserved as time goes by. They are the heroes.

Al Zdon
2002

CONTENTS

A TENT CITY AT CAMP STONE, MARYLAND

The headquarters for Gen. Gorman and his staff was along the Potomac. It's possible that the sergeant major, third from right, is Ed Davis.

Photos from the Collection of the Minnesota Historical Society.

THE FIRST MINNESOTA
AT BULL RUN

The First Minnesota was the first regiment to be tendered to the Union at the outbreak of the Civil War in 1861. Ed Davis signed up with the St. Paul Pioneer Guards, later one of the 10 companies comprising the First Minnesota. His letters paint a vivid picture of the early days of the war and the Battle of Bull Run where the First Minnesota was one of the few units to distinguish itself on the field of battle.

Work was not going well for Ed Davis in his adopted hometown of St. Paul in April of 1861. A railroad surveyor by profession, he was 25 years old and unemployed. He wrote home to New York about his prospects, "Everything in the future now looks dark and uncertain."

That concern with his personal future, though, was overshadowed in his letters by descriptions of the war fever sweeping through St. Paul. On April 9, he reported a rumor he had heard that the soldiers at Fort Snelling had been ordered to Washington D.C., and that the St. Paul Pioneer Guards, a state militia unit, was to be ordered to Ft. Ridgley on the Minnesota River.

Indeed, on April 13, in the wake of the firing on Ft. Sumpter, the Pioneer Guard unit held a meeting and the members signed a paper agreeing to enlist in federal service when the call came forth.

Gov. Alexander Ramsey was on business that day in Washington D.C. and had tendered a regiment from Minnesota to President Lincoln, the first state to offer troops in the developing crisis.

In a letter to his father on April 13, Davis said there was "intense excitement" in the war news, "and we shall await with some anxiety the telegraphs of tomorrow."

"I regret civil war as much as anyone," he wrote. "But if all accounts are true, the Southerners richly deserve the 'dressing' they will receive." He concluded his letter, "My health is very good, and if I had constant employment, I might be contented."

On April 16, the official call for volunteers did go out from Gov. Ramsey's office. The governor requested one regiment of 10 companies with 100 men in each company. The call was received with enthusiastic support around the state.

Ed Davis didn't hesitate. He immediately went down and joined the Pioneer Guards. "The news has caused great excitement," he wrote his brother, "and the Stars and Stripes are not only floating from all the places of business and public buildings, but even the private houses all over town are adorned with them."

"This City is unanimous for the Union." He also told his brother that he hopes "the South gets whipped quicker than lightning."

Davis had served earlier in the 7th New York Regiment and was an experienced soldier. He talked about a commission in his letter, but concluded that, "I'd rather serve as a private." His enlistment was for three months.

The Pioneer Guards drilled daily in the St. Paul Armory and on the streets of the city. "I am even at this late day better drilled than the best of them," Davis wrote home. "I could even learn the officers their tactics."

Despite his prowess at military life, Davis was somewhat bitter to find that he was only being made a corporal. "I am willing to serve my country in any capacity, but this treatment is different from what I expected."

The First Minnesota was assembled and sworn in at Ft. Snelling on April 29, 1861. The old fort was in a state of disuse, and the men spent some time getting it ready. They were served a good dinner that night on rough boards using tin plates and tin cups.

The men had no uniforms, but were issued a blanket, a red flannel shirt and a pair of stockings. The shirts had been purchased hurriedly at various stores in St. Paul. Some of the units had brought Springfield rifles with them, and others were issued .69 caliber muskets from the state armory.

Davis was assigned as a corporal to Company A, and he confided in a letter that the new officers assigned were lacking in military experience and "about as inefficient set of men as could be found."

The drilling went on daily. On May 7th, Davis wrote: "I have been hard at work day after day drilling the boys."

He was transferred from the St. Paul Company to the Wabasha volunteers, Company I, and was acting as the company's orderly, in charge of much of the paperwork that had to be done.

"We have been given comfortable quarters and plenty to eat," he wrote. He also had information that six of the

companies would be sent off to garrison duty at regional forts in order to free up the regular army troops stationed there to be sent back East.

"The boys protest against any such proceedings, and say they did not enlist to fortify the forts in the state," he wrote. "They cannot see how they can defend the Constitution when occupying a fort, even on the Red River."

Davis said he enjoyed the group of men from Wabasha, "as good a lot of young fellows as could be found."

On May 7th, the men were asked to re-enlist for three years, or the duration of the war, rather than the three months they had originally signed up for. The request was not greeted with enthusiasm by Company I.

"The boys are dissatisfied with their officers, and I think with some reason." Davis said the men would sign on for three years if the present officers would resign, but they had declined to do so. Some of the men, including Davis, asked to be discharged so they could join the Stillwater company, but the request was denied.

Many of the men eventually did sign on for the three-year hitch, but many others had had their taste of army life and went home. Their ranks were quickly filled by new recruits eager to join the regiment and go to war.

On May 9th, the regiment was issued black felt hats and black pantaloons to complete their wardrobe. The Winona company, though, kept their splendid gray uniforms that had been presented to them by the people of Winona.

On May 21, the regiment was marched to Nicollet Island in Minneapolis for a banquet given in their honor. On May 24,

AFTER THE RETREAT FROM BULL RUN
the First Minnesota took up residence at Camp Stone, Maryland, along the Potomac River. Many of the men returned from the battle with only the clothes on their backs.

they marched to the Capitol to receive a state flag from the women of St. Paul. They then participated in a banquet in their honor at the Winslow House.

Fort Snelling was a beehive of activity in those weeks, always full of relatives, friends and visitors who came to see the regiment drill and to bring them items of support.

A typical day for the soldiers began at 5 a.m. with roll call. Sick call was at 6:30 with breakfast at 7:30. The company drilled from 8-10 a.m. and then joined the rest of the regiment for a drill from 10 to 11:30.

Lunch was at 12:30 p.m., company drill from 2-4 p.m., regimental drill until 5:30, and supper at 6:30. There was a dress parade at 7, roll calls at 7:30 p.m. and 9 p.m. followed by lights out.

As expected, two companies each were sent off to Ft. Ripley, north of St. Cloud, to Ft. Ridgley on the Minnesota River, and to Fort Abercrombie on the Red River to relieve the Army troops. Four companies, including Davis' Company I, stayed at Fort Snelling.

Davis was proud of his comrades. "The boys are getting settled down in to something like soldiers. This is as fine a regiment as has ever been mustered into service, and a fighting one at that." But the drilling was "monotonous. I shall be glad when we get started off South."

Davis had heard of a grand master plan where the Federal army would soon number some 500,000 men and would march through the South from three points of the compass by early Fall of 1861.

By early June, Davis was promoted to a sergeant major of the regiment, the highest enlisted rank, but he still hoped for eventual promotion to the officer ranks. "When we get into active service, I shall either get killed or get promoted."

On June 14, the First Minnesota received orders to Washington D.C., and the camp was filled with joy. The men were awakened to the news, and they didn't bother getting dressed, but rushed around hurrahing loudly and hugging each other.

The companies who were stationed at the outlying forts were recalled. The men of Company E, worried they might miss the movement to Washington, marched all night from Ft. Ripley to rejoin the regiment.

The regiment left Fort Snelling on June 22 at 6 a.m. on two steamboats to take them down the Mississippi River to meet the nearest railroad lines. Davis was on board the Northern Belle and the boat stopped at Hastings, Red

A GROUP OF OFFICERS

in the First Minnesota Regiment had their photo taken by famed Civil War photographer Matthew Brady near Edwards Ferry, Maryland, on March 16, 1862.

Wing, Wabasha and Winona along the way so the young men could say goodbye to their families and friends. "The scenes of parting were truly affecting."

In a letter to his father, Davis recalled his thoughts as the boat left Winona. "As the moon rose above the bluffs behind the town, we bid farewell to Minnesota to which place all of us can never hope to return."

The men reached LaCrosse at 11 p.m. that night, and were transferred to railway cars for the journey to Chicago where they arrived the next evening. They marched through town, and the Chicago Tribune wrote, "They are unquestionably the finest body of troops that has yet appeared on our streets."

Onward they traveled to Pittsburgh and Harrisburg, greeted all along the way by cheering crowds waving handkerchiefs and flags at the young soldiers. "It was a perfect ovation," Davis wrote.

Even when the train neared Washington D.C. and entered areas considered loyal to the South, the reception was still warm. "The enthusiasm was just as great, especially among the ladies. The Minnesota First is truly a good looking body of men."

The reception in Baltimore, though, was not quite so cordial. A hostile throng quietly lined the street as the regiment marched from one train station to another. "We marched through the city with guns loaded and capped."

"The boys would have given a good account of themselves had they been molested."

They arrived in Washington late at night on June 26 and were quartered in churches in the city. The next day, they moved to a camp a half mile east of the Capital, and on July 3, were marched to new quarters across the Potomac near Alexandria, Virginia. The Fifth Massachusetts was bivouacked on one side, and the 6th Pennsylvania on the other side. "We allow no one in our camp, and none of the boys are allowed to go out."

"There are quite a number of successionists about four miles from us strongly entrenched," Davis wrote. The weather was "hot and sultry." He noted that Confederate Gen. Beauregard had been threatening Washington D.C. with his troops, but "He is as near Washington as he will ever get with an army."

Davis had a tent of his own, one of perquisites of his rank, and he was situated about 25 feet from Col. Gorman, the regiment's top officer. As a sergeant major, he wore blue pants and a gray, flannel shirt. He carried no arms except a sword and a pistol, "and I find them enough."

By July 8th, the Second Michigan and the New York Fire Zouaves had joined the camp near Alexandria, swelling the population of the area to over 5,000 men. The weather had taken a turn toward summer. "The heat is almost intolerable."

Life in camp was dreary, and the drilling was tedious. "The greatest caution to be taken is in health and I avoid all liquors of every kind, cold tea and coffee being preferable to anything else. I regret to say that many of our boys are given to intoxication."

Davis wrote that the highlight of every day was the mail call.

He speculated in a letter to his father what the upcoming action would be like. "A short and bloody fight's to many of us preferable to a protracted residence in this country where two hostile armies are gaping at one another." He compared the standoff to a couple of school boys daring each other to fight.

"The boys are not afraid, and all they want is orders and they will be to Fairfax (Court House) in one night, and to Manassas the next day ready to do or die."

On July 14, the men were ordered to place three days rations in their haversacks, pack up 40 rounds of ammunition and a blanket, and get ready to travel. "I have no doubt that our progress through Virginia will be obstinately contested," Davis wrote. He noted the rumor that the Southern army was not allowed to have newspapers in camp, a sure sign to him that the Confederates didn't believe in their cause. He expected victory by spring, and used several handwritten sheets of letter paper on expounding his bravado about the situation.

"Many of us will leave our bones in Southern soil, but they will die in a holy and noble cause and in defense of the only flag worth dying for — the Stars and Stripes."

On July 16th, they finally began the slow trek south, leaving their knapsacks packed and in their tents. Ten men from each company were left behind to guard the camp. The road to Fairfax Court House was 16 miles long and crowded with troops, wagons, artillery and hundreds of spectators from Washington who had come down to see the battle.

By the 19th, they were in Centreville, just about three miles from Bull Run and five miles from Manassas Junction. The Union's ultimate objective was Richmond, but the short-term goal was to push the Confederate Army back and give Washington D.C. some breathing room.

There were about 35,000 Federals on the field, the largest army ever assembled in North America to that point, under the direction of Gen. Irvin McDowell. The Rebels had about 20,000 men, under Gen. P.G.T. Beauregard, but reinforcements were arriving on the railway system at Manassas by the hour.

The First Minnesota was on the far right of the Union attack, and crossed Bull Run early in the morning on July 21 at Sudley Ford. The plan was for the Union forces to wheel around and hit the Confederates hard from the northwest.

The battle went well for the Union through the morning and they captured several hills from the Southern forces as they drove them back. Victory seemed almost in sight, with the road to Richmond open and waiting.

About 2 p.m., the tide of battle turned, though. The Federals brought two batteries to the top of Henry House Hill. Ricketts' Battery was supported by the First Minnesota. The Federals were unaware that a very large Southern force was in the woods just 80 or 100 yards from where the artillery was set up.

Ricketts Battery came up through the middle of the Minnesotans, splitting the regiment in two for the remainder of the battle. As the guns were just beginning to fire, the Confederates attacked. The Minnesotans and other units held off the ferocious attack, including point blank blasts of canister and grape from Southern artillery. Three times the Rebels captured the Federal guns, and three times the Union troops recaptured them — twice by the First Minnesota. Finally, with a pause in the action, it looked like the Federals had won the day. There were "huzzahs" of triumph at Henry House Hill.

Despite the temporary victory, the Union regiments were disorganized and also very thirsty by this time. Many of the men had gone to fill their canteens, and others had gone souvenir hunting. Many others were just overcome by the long and hot day. When the Rebels came again, the First Minnesota was forced to fall back with the other Union regiments.

The Minnesotans marched through Centreville all the way to Alexandria, and after a few hours sleep, were awakened to march into Washington D.C.

Ed Davis wrote a letter to his brother on July 23, probably as soon as he had a chance after the long march. "We were in the thickest of the fight," he began.

He praised the regiment and reported that the Minnesotans had continually and cooly fired, reloaded and fired again despite being under heavy fire from "thousands of the enemy within 100 feet of us."

"No soldiers in the world could stand such a fire as we experienced, and so we retreated. We are cut almost to pieces."

Davis said in that letter written hours after the battle that over 400 of the regiment were killed or wounded. Those figures were exaggerated, but the First Minnesota did suffer the highest casualty rate of any unit in the battle with 42 killed, 108 wounded and 30 missing in action — fully 20 percent of the men engaged at Bull Run.

Davis survived with no major wounds, but his description of rain of fire on Henry House is harrowing:

"I have, thank God, escaped unhurt with but one scratch during the action. I wear a sword scabbard of heavy copper. A bullet struck it within 1/4 inch of its top indenting it so much that I could only put the point of my sword in. 1/2 inch higher, and it might have gone through my body. Another bullet struck the scabbard about midway bending it out to nearly a right angle. Another took my pistol holder clean off my belt. While another took a small piece from the top of my ear."

Davis described one incident when the Minnesotans were attacked by Confederate cavalry. "I picked up my revolver,

FORT SNELLING
was in a state of disrepair when troops began arriving to train for the Civil War duty in 1861.

AFTER MUSTERING IN,
the officers of the First Minnesota posed in front of the commandant's house at Ft. Snelling in May 1861.

and when the cavalry made its charge, I fired my shots then threw my revolver at them and broke for the woods. I think I was the last of our regiment (alive) to leave. When I went over the fence they were not 50 feet behind me and the bullets were whistling about my head like rain. How I escaped, I don't know."

Davis wrote that after the First Minnesota's second charge, when they held the hill for a time, the regiment was only able to muster 450 men. As the Confederates counter-attacked, Col. Heinzelman rode up to Col. Gorman and said, "Good day, officer. Take your men from the field or they will all be slaughtered."

The regiment retreated, much to the chagrin of Davis. "I was on the field till the battle was over, and I never was so mortified as when I heard that our army was in full retreat. I wished at that moment that I had left my body there."

The next day, July 24, as the regiment took up temporary quarters in Washington, Davis had time to write a longer letter to his brother with more details about the battle.

He describes how the First Minnesota had left Centreville about 2 a.m. the morning of the battle. Davis filled his canteen with cold coffee, and left his blanket behind.

By 9 a.m., they could hear the battle, and an hour later they were near the scene of the fighting. They filled their canteens with water "almost unfit for cattle" and marched quick time and then double quick time to the front, seeing many dead and wounded along the way.

The men stripped off their haversacks and blankets, "throwing them aside as we advanced, retaining nothing but our arms, accoutrements and canteens."

After this quick advance, the regiment was then ordered to wait for the arrival of Ricketts' artillery pieces. Davis checked his men. "I passed through the lines and found everyone in good spirits and anxious to take a hand in."

The men advanced in four ranks on the extreme left of the enemy in an attempt to turn the Confederate left flank and, after a two mile hike, "The cannon balls and shells were flying thick and fast, fortunately most of them over our heads."

The Minnesotans marched up Henry House Hill and formed a line of battle. "The battery was miserably placed," Davis wrote. He informed Col. Gorman that the enemy was within 100 yards of their position, but Gorman mistakenly thought the men in the nearby woods were Union soldiers. Davis argued otherwise, but Gorman

replied, "No, sir, they are our friends. I depend on you to form the left wing."

Confusion was the rule of the day. The Union and Confederate troops were not yet outfitted in the blue and gray that became traditional. For instance, the First Minnesota and the Alabama regiment they faced that day both wore red shirts. The Virginians, next to the Alabamans in the line, wore blue uniforms. And, of course, the First Minnesota's Winona company was still attired in its gray uniforms.

Adding to the mess was the fact that the Confederate flag carried at this battle looked a lot like the U.S. flag from a distance.

Davis went down the line, readying the men, and saw clearly that the soldiers in the woods were not friendly troops. "Without waiting for the Colonel, I ordered 'Fire and load lying.'" Just as a hail of bullets exploded from the woods, the Minnesotans hit the ground and began firing at the enemy, reloading four times before retreating from that exposed position.

The First Minnesota at that point received help from the New York Fire Zouaves on the left, and Davis tried to rally his troops. Again, though, Col. Gorman intervened. "Cease firing, they are our friends," he ordered. The men stopped firing and were rewarded by another hail of gunfire from the woods, and a charge of Confederate troops.

Again the Minnesotans fell back. Davis and the officers formed ranks "without regard to company, and up we went again over the hill." Once again, they were forced to back off. "We retired in good order, firing as we went."

Davis wrote that at that point of the battle he hoped the Union troops were merely reorganizing for another attack, but he soon realized that the orderly retreat by the Union army was becoming a rout. "It was indeed a terrible sight."

"I thought then and I think now we were betrayed by our generals. We had no reserves, nothing to rally on."

Davis recounted the retreat back to Alexandria and Washington, "the last 18 miles in heavy rain." The men had had nothing to eat for nearly two days. Davis, himself, was destitute. "I have lost everything but my clothes."

The First Minnesota kept in marching order as they left the battlefield. "Minnesota need never be ashamed of her sons. No troops were more brave or courageous or stood their ground under such a murderous fire."

Later, Davis was congratulated by Col. Gorman. "The conduct of none of my officers affords me more satisfaction then did yours, and I thank you for it."

Though small compared to later battles, the Battle of Bull Run, or Manassas as the South called it, was a bloody encounter. The CSA lost 387 killed, 1,582 wounded and 13 missing. The U.S. lost 470 killed, 1,071 wounded and 1,793 missing.

The Southern army was too beat up to mount a successful attempt to attack the retreating Union troops, but the battle was a wake-up call for the Union and the hundreds of idle spectators who rode their buggies into the Virginia countryside. It was going to be a long war.

After the battle, the first Minnesota was ordered to Camp Stone, northwest of Washington along the Potomac River in Maryland. The regiment took part in nearly every major battle until it was mustered out in 1864 at the end of its three-year enlistment. The regiment became famous for its charge at Gettysburg where it encountered over 80 percent in casualties.

Charles Edward Davis did get promoted, as he had hoped. He served as second lieutenant in Company I, first lieutenant in Company A and captain in Company E. He was discharged on May 5, 1864, never having suffered a serious wound.

Davis returned to St. Paul where he continued his career as a railroad surveyor. He died on May 10, 1886, at the age of 50.

Editor's Note: This story was taken mainly from the personal letters of Charles Edward Davis in the collection of the Minnesota Historical Society, and the account of the First Minnesota Volunteer Regiment in Minnesota in the Civil and Indian Wars, 1861-1865, *published in 1889.*

Special thanks to Stephen Osman, director of the Ft. Snelling History Center.

A SMOKE BREAK AT THE GATLING GUN

One of Lewis Burlingham's comrades, Bob Coles, takes a pipe break on the gunner's seat of a one-inch Gatling gun in the Phillipines.

LETTERS FROM THE PHILIPPINES

The Spanish-American War was America's first military action since the Civil War, and young Lewis P. Burlingham of Stillwater was eager to fight for his country. A year later, as part of the 13th Minnesota Regiment on duty in the Philippines, the euphoria was replaced by a longing for home and a bitterness about U.S. policy against the native Filipinos as the war dragged on and on.

Lewis Burlingham was a young lad of 19 when he signed up with the First Regiment of the National Guard of the State of Minnesota on April 29, 1898. He had to get a permission slip from his parents to join.

He was 5 feet 6 and one-half inches in his stocking feet, and as thin as a rail. He joined his older brother, Will, who had been in the regiment for some time.

Burlingham, who grew up in Stillwater, was caught up in the war fever that was sweeping the nation. America was taking on Spain in both Cuba and the Philippines, and there had been a call to arms.

It was the first major military action for the U.S. since the Civil War.

Minnesota Governor D.M. Clough had been notified by President William McKinley on April 25, 1898, that Minnesota was to supply three regiments to take on the foe. The First Regiment of the National Guard became the 13th Minnesota in the federal scheme of things.

Men were called from Minneapolis, St. Paul, Red Wing, Stillwater and St. Cloud to fill out the regiment. Gen. Charles Reeve, who had been running the First Regiment since 1892, was the first com-

manding officer of the new federal unit.

The men were gathered and reviewed on the morning of April 29 at the State Capitol in St. Paul before an enthusiastic crowd. In 1898, it was still the Old Capitol on Wabasha between 10th and Exchange in St. Paul. They then marched to the state's fairgrounds, which had been renamed Camp Ramsey in honor of Minnesota's Civil War governor, Alexander Ramsey.

The men were quartered in the horse and cow barns of the fairgrounds.

Burlingham wrote his first letters from Camp Ramsey, and told his mother that everything was going great, although conditions were a little crowded in the horse stall he shared with three other privates. He nearly always signed his letters, "I remain, your loving son, Lewis."

"We're having a great time here. For breakfast we have bread, coffee, meat and potatoes," he wrote on May 2. "When one of us wants to turn over, he has to holler and the rest of us turn at the same time."

The men were equipped with hats, blouses, overalls and blankets at the camp. On May 7, they were officially mustered in as active duty Federal troops. The Twin City Mandolin and Guitar Club serenaded the young men as they went through the mustering-in ceremony.

Burlingham and his compatriots drilled for five hours a day. In between and during the drilling, the troops were host to thousands of visitors who came to see our brave Minnesota boys get ready for war. The visitors brought food and other gifts that were much appreciated by the soldiers. A fund of $15,000 was collected for the benefit of the troops as they headed off to war.

Gov. Clough was told by the federal authorities that he had to select one of Minnesota's three regiments to go to war. The other two were to be sent to Chickamauga National Park in Georgia for stateside duty.

He picked the First Regiment, and there was great rejoicing in the cattle barns that night. Nobody had joined up just to go to Chickamauga.

On May 16, the boys of the 13th Minnesota left for California. On the numerous stops along the way, the Minnesotans were often greeted by the town folks who showered them with fruit and other food and sometimes flowers.

In a diary he only kept sporadically, Burlingham noted with thankfulness the gifts from "the ladies of Colfax" and the "ladies of Auburn" as the train passed through the small California towns.

The 13th Minnesota arrived at Camp Merritt in San Francisco and "we pitched our tents in the rain."

The training schedule resumed, and on June 18, the 13th Minnesota performed a review for the Red Cross and for the local people. A local newspaper wrote, "Very fine men, these Minnesota boys, well-equipped and excellently drilled. They are an example of what volunteers can be, and are surpassed by very few regulars."

On June 21, 1898, Burlingham wrote his mother in Stillwater that the Minnesotans had received the rest of their uniform including blue trousers, shoes, flannel shirts, underwear, socks, suspenders and rubber blankets. He also told her that it looked like the regiment might be leaving soon because their ammunition had been put aboard their troop transport, "The City of Para."

As they were doing their last preparations, they were sent a message by the Army leader, Major General Wesley Merritt. The general told the troops that he had especially requested the Minnesota regiment for action in the Philippines.

Burlingham wrote a comforting postcard about himself and brother Will to his worried mother on June 25th. "Both of us are well and gaining weight. We are working hard packing up."

< LEWIS BURLINGHAM

shown after his service in the 13th Minnesota when he was a member of the Minnesota Home Guard.

> AS A CIVILIAN

Burlingham worked for a wallpaper company and then a printing firm in the Twin Cities.

On June 27, the men climbed on board the City of Para.

The ocean voyage lasted 42 days and was a miserable experience for Burlingham and the others. The food was bad, there was a shortage of water, and the monotony of the sea voyage was deathly.

Burlingham managed to get accommodations in a state room, but suffered with the poor food. "I manage to buy a meal from one of the porters at times."

The ship arrived at Manila harbor on August 7, and the 13th Minnesota, made its home at Camp Dewey, on the south side of the city. The Spanish forces still controlled most of the city.

The American Fleet, under Admiral Dewey, had already destroyed the Spanish Fleet in Manila harbor (from which came the famous phrase, "You may fire when ready, Gridley"). There had been a slow build-up of American troops outside Manila.

Burlingham wrote home: "We bought bamboo beds from the natives. The ants here are a great deal worse than the mosquitoes, and goodness knows they were bad enough."

The rain poured down on the American troops. "It rained all night," Burlingham wrote. "I couldn't sleep. You couldn't account for there being so much mud and water and rain to contend with. Oh, this is a hot country. I wouldn't give a hip hip hooray for the whole cheese."

Over the next few days, the Minnesotans had a chance to go up to the breastworks, the furthest advance of the American Army. They looked on at the entrenched enemy, just a few hundred yards away.

With the arrival of the Minnesota troops and others, the third expeditionary force to land in the Philippines, the U.S. high command had enough troops to press home the final attack. On August 13th, the major advance on Manila was launched. Ships in the harbor opened fire on the Spanish fortifications.

The 13th Minnesota, under the command of Gen. Arthur MacArthur, the father of the World War II hero, marched toward the Spanish lines on the right or west side of the front. Each man was equipped with haversack, a gun, a canteen and 100 rounds of ammunition.

The Spanish fell back before the American assault, but laid down a withering fire as they retreated. Burlingham sent a map home to his mother showing the advance of the 13th Minnesota. On it he wrote notes:

-- "Bugler Patterson was killed here."

GATHERING FOR SUPPER, members of the 13th Minnesota Regiment crowd around a table at "an outpost of Colonade on Paso." The unit spent much of its time in the Philippines on provost duty in the city of Manila.

-- "This was one of the hot places. Bullets were coming fast upon this road."

-- And further on. "This was the hottest place of the day. This was the place where Captain Bomstad was shot through the lungs."

Burlingham later wrote that at one point he was in the forefront of the American troops and a bullet from the friendly troops at his rear whizzed by his head, hit a wall, and dropped at his feet. "It was more annoying than all the Spanish bullets flying by, some very close, as a regular was shot down at my side... You could almost feel the bullets whiz by your head." He kept the bullet for a souvenir.

The attack was launched at noon, and the battle was won by 1:35 in the afternoon. Company K, made up of the Stillwater men including Lewis and Will, captured the outlying town of Cingalon and then headed toward the harbor where they camped out that night in the suburb of Malate.

The Minnesotans lost four men and had 33 wounded in the attack. "That was a miracle," Burlingham wrote, "the way the bullets flew."

Instead of pressing forward, though, the Minnesota unit was left in Manila to be the provost-guard of the city. From August 20 until March 19, 1899, the Minnesotans policed the city, a duty that chaffed at some of the young lads who didn't come all the way to the Philippines to be city policemen.

In fact, an unusual form of desertion began to take place. The men would leave their guard posts when nobody was looking and head out to the front lines to fight with their peers from other states. The practice was stopped when two Minnesotans from D Company were wounded in a skirmish on the front lines.

Burlingham's first letter home after the big battle was on August 21. He told his mom about how the Filipino freedom fighters, called Insurgents by the Americans, had captured 2,000 Spanish soldiers. "They are starving them to death, and when they get the chance, they would cut their heads off. The Spanish are more to be pitied than to be scorned."

As the weeks dragged on, some bad morale crept into Company K. Burlingham told his mother that the troops were especially unhappy about a $500 fund that had been collected for the Stillwater men in their hometown. "It needs to be taken out of the hands of the officers. All it is used for is food, cigars and liquor for the different officers. Please do not hint that I wrote this to you, as the officers might get in on it and make things and life misery for me."

One officer in particular, referred to derisively as "Fighting Joe, the Albino King" drew the special wrath of Burlingham. "He is a fool and doesn't know the first thing about what he should do and what he should not do for the company."

Burlingham said he was torn between keeping his pay or sending it home. "I could keep it here and use it to keep from starving when we didn't have anything to eat but hardtack and coffee."

"I'm going to see if I can't get to town as I can take a bath and get some cork insoles as my feet are all blistered from the march out here on the cobblestones."

But life wasn't all bad for the occupying forces. Company K's 106 men were quartered in Manila's walled city. "We now have all kinds of music in our quarters," he wrote on September 18. "The boys all put in money for a fiddle and guitar, and they paid the rent on a piano."

He also noted that some of the volunteers had monkeys as pets.

On September 30, he told his mother: "Manila isn't such an unhealthy place now as it has been cleaned up pretty well and put most of the smell out."

By October 16, the garrison duty was getting to

Burlingham, and he called the Philippines "this beastly country. I hope they get us out of here as quickly as possible. We are all anxious to get out of here and back to good old America where the climate is healthy and not full of all sorts of diseases which are constantly spreading and causing more trouble than the Spanish bullets." It was especially galling that the two Minnesota regiments that had been sent to Chickamauga had already been mustered out of service.

A few days later, he wrote that brother Will was sick and had been hospitalized for three days. "No need to worry about Bill, you can't down him, he is too bull-headed."

He reported that he and his mates were chipping in to buy an oil stove as the cooler weather set in. They were also pooling their resources to buy better food. "You can bet we are going to make the best of it while we are here."

On December 2nd, his letter was full of more complaints about the officers. He also said many of the boys were getting colds. "I take quinine to prevent me from getting one. Pretty smart ain't I?"

Rumors were sweeping through the 13th Minnesota about going home. On December 15th, the Astor Battery, a unit the Minnesotans had shared a ship with on the way over, was sent home. The men hoped they would be relieved by the regular Army in January.

On Christmas Day, a dinner that was shipped all the way from Stillwater was presented to Company K. It had been prepared by the George Crook W.R.C. No. 103 of Stillwater and included shrimp salad, roast chicken, mashed potatoes, cranberry sauce, cookies, pie, mixed nuts and cigars.

On New Year's Day, a field day was held in Manila for all the troops with sports activities and entertainment. The 13th Minnesota took on the 10th Pennsylvania in a football game. The evening's program included singing, a "black face specialty," a contortionist, and a play called the "Fall of Adam and Eve."

The new year brought no change for the Minnesotans, but a great change to Burlingham's letters. Gone were the happy notes and braggadocio of earlier days, replaced by a longing to go home and disgust with the present situation.

And he had other bad news. At some point in January, his fiancee returned his ring and a gift watch to Burlingham's parents.

"I felt so bad over the sad news I read about my sweetheart," he wrote on January 30th, 1899. He put up a brave front. "Don't worry about your boys, they can take care of themselves." But ended the letter with a cry for help. "I will go crazy if we have to stay here much longer."

The political scene had changed dramatically in the Philippines, and the Insurgents, who had been the allies of the U.S. during the Spanish occupation, now saw the Americans as another foreign country trying to take over their soil. The Insurgents had been very unhappy when the Americans would not share the occupation of Manila with them. The bad feeling soon evolved into open hostilities under the leadership of Emilio Aguinaldo.

Burlingham wrote in his diary: "We had our first battle with the insurgents on February 4. Firing commenced at 9:30 p.m. and we were kept in arms all night."

In a letter written on February 6, he gave more details. "Well, at last we have run up against the Philippinos and they have got the worst of it. Although our killed and wounded is supposed, at this time, to be quite heavy." He called the action, "fast, fierce and furious."

The Americans drove the insurgent forces out from the city into the neighboring mountains. "The Americans set fire to everything they came to and then shot the occupants as they came out. All around Manila looks like a human slaughterhouse of natives piled up in windrows four and five deep and covered with blood."

Another major uprising was put down by the Minnesotans and others on February 22, with heavy fighting on the north side of Manila.

The 13th Minnesota was finally relieved of police duty on March 18. Burlingham wrote home on March 21 that the boys were "camped in our little dog tents" next to the Luneta River. The troops were excited, and there was an anticipation of a major offensive.

"We expect to go out in a flying column, rout all the (insurgents) in a hurry, come back and go home. The Gugus haven't much powder or bullets left, and they are slowly starving."

On March 22, the Minnesotans broke camp and marched to Manila's reservoir to protect the city's water source. For the next few days, the 13th participated in the Battle of Mariquina. "We had quite a quarrel with the (insurgents) and the bullets were flying fast and thick over our heads, but we drove them three or four miles back." The men slept in the open air, he wrote, "with the bullets still singing over our heads."

The 13th Minnesota was loaded on a train that took them to Marilao where they guarded the track for some days.

Soon they were part of a larger operation that began on April 22nd and aimed at pushing the insurgents back.

On the 23rd, the troops took on the rebels near the town of Norzagaray, driving them out of their trenches, through the town, and across a river. In the action, Sergeant Will Burlingham was severely wounded in the leg as he led his men in the charge.

Marching and fighting, Company K helped the Americans capture dozens of villages, burn 15,000 bushels of rice that had been hidden by the insurgents, and finally push the rebels back past the city of San Isidro. In 33 days, the 13th Minnesota marched over 130 miles, helped capture 28 towns and suffered one killed, nine wounded, and had 77 men disabled, mostly by disease.

In a long letter on June 1, Lewis Burlingham let his bottled up emotions run over the pages. "I suppose you have heard the unlucky news about Will," he began the letter, but soon shifted into a blistering attack on American policy. "From letters and newspaper talk you may think that they are an inferior class of people we are fighting against. We are not fighting women and children or bows and arrows. We are fighting against odds and big odds."

Burlingham told his parents that the insurgents had better weapons than the Americans, bigger cannons, and "They know the country by heart." He said there had been "glory in fighting against Spain," but there was no glory now. "It's all done for greed."

"You are all in the dark. You are all blindfolded. You think

SANDBAGGED FORTIFICATIONS
were in place at high points around the city of Manila. The 13th Minnesota was stationed in the city for many months in 1898-99.

your sons are fighting for a good cause, but you know nothing, absolutely nothing.

"This war here is nothing more than a damn political and religious affair and has cost the lives of 2,000 good American men to be laid away forever or else crippled for life. Your eldest son is amongst the most unfortunate ones."

Page after page of anger poured out. "I'm tired of being a soft mark for some of these high-minded, white-whiskered generals and politicians."

He described the action the 13th Minnesota had encountered. The unit broke camp on April 22nd at Bigaa, and headed for the mountains. The next day, Will was hit.

"He was going down a hill and had just stepped up on a rice paddy to go down to the next one when he was hit, and, of course, it swung him around and he fell forward on his shoulder over the paddy which jarred him considerably with his load on his shoulders. He was then dressed and taken back to the ambulance where I first saw him as soon as I had heard of it."

Will Burlingham had been struck by a bullet that entered his left leg just below the knee cap, passed through the bone, and exited out the back of his leg. Lewis told his parents that he feared Will would have a "still knee" from the wound.

Lewis made it through the campaign unscathed, except for his health. "I had the quick-step and was as thin as a three-cornered file as I wasn't able to eat a thing."

In a letter on May 15, he mentioned that he had been able to take souvenirs from a rebel he had shot. He also said he had quit his clerk's job, and was now standing guard duty. "Will is up and walking around with a cane and a splint on his leg."

On June 7, Burlingham asked his mother to air out his clothes to get them ready for his return. "I have a bad cold this morning, and I am nervous, but I guess it will wear off all night."

On July 3rd, Will was sent home on a transport. Lewis wrote home, "I am alive and that's all I can say for myself." The 13th Minnesota spent two more months on guard duty before being relieved. A witness at the time said the troops were "thin, hardened, ragged, bearded and a rough looking crowd." They embarked on the USS Sheridan on August 10 and on the 7th of September, the ship pulled into San Francisco Bay.

In his last letter, Burlingham told his parents that he had weighed 133 lbs. when he left for overseas, and he now weighed 122 and a half. "Oh, Lord, I wish I was home so I

THE SPANISH-AMERICAN WAR

Though it only lasted 10 weeks, the Spanish-American War played a critical role in the development of the United States as a world power. Throughout the 19th Century, European nations ruled the world. The United States had its Monroe Doctrine, which forbid interference in the Western Hemisphere, but had little military or economic might to enforce the doctrine. As the century closed, though, the U.S. grew in might.

A longstanding quarrel between the U.S. and Spain over Spanish governance of Cuba and Puerto Rico erupted into war when an American ship, the USS Maine, blew up in Havana Harbor in early 1898. The great newspapers of the day also colored the events to help push the nation into war.

The U.S. and Spain fought several actions in Cuba, including Teddy Roosevelt leading his Roughriders up San Juan Hill. In the end, the U.S. soundly defeated the Spanish forces in Cuba.

In the Pacific, Admiral Dewey led his Great White Fleet (which had been painted battle gray) to an attack of the Spanish fleet in Manila Harbor. It was a great victory for the Americans, and ended Spain's role as a world sea power.

American troops, including the 13th Minnesota, were sent to the Philippines to take on the Spanish, and in the Battle of Manila on August 13, 1898, the U.S. won handily.

The fighting continued, however, when the Filipinos realized that the U.S. had simply replaced Spain as a colonial power. It wasn't until the middle of 1899 that the insurgent forces were suppressed, and the U.S. ruled over its new empire. The American Century had begun.

wouldn't have to write letters."

They were mustered out in California, given two months' extra pay, and arrived back home in Minnesota to a heroes' reception on October 12. They led a huge parade down Nicollet Avenue in Minneapolis as President William McKinley and members of his cabinet looked on.

The 13th Minnesota had lost 44 men, including seven who died in battle and two who were missing in action. Many had died of illness and disease, two had been killed in accidents, one had drowned, and one man had deserted.

Lewis Burlingham, who had received $172.04 for his final military paycheck, and the others in Company K were welcomed home to Stillwater with a parade, a banquet at the Opera House and a Grand Military Ball.

Burlingham's discharge papers noted his "honest and faithful service."

He married Sophie Johnson in 1902 and they moved to St. Paul where he worked in the wallpaper department at Schuneman's Department Store. The couple later moved to Minneapolis where he worked for the Miller Davis Printing Co.

He was a sergeant in the Home Guard during World War I, and he tried desperately to join the American forces for the Great War, but he was rejected by each of the branches of service for a physical condition. He finally joined the YMCA and served in France as a civilian.

In 1924, he was awarded a $12 a month pension as a Spanish-American War veteran for an unspecified condition.

Through the years, he stayed very active in the 13th Minnesota Regiment Association, and was credited in later years with keeping the organization going as its secretary. The veterans of the 13th Minnesota held a reunion every August 13, the anniversary of the Battle of Manila.

He died June 3rd, 1951, at the age of 72.

Several sources were used for this story, the most important of which was the collection of letters and other papers of Lewis P. Burlingham at the Minnesota Historical Society. Other sources were:

— *Minnesota in the Spanish American War and the Philippine Insurrection*. Edited by Frankly Holbrook, 1923.

— *The 13th Minnesota Volunteer Infantry, First Regiment, National Guard State of Minnesota*, by Norris W. Brown, 1900.

— *The Spanish-American War*, by Deborah Bachrach, Lucent Books, 1991.

THE LAST LIVING FOUNDER

George Washington Bentley lived to be 101 years old and was the last living person who had been present at the founding of The American Legion in Paris in 1919.

Photos are from the collection of the Bentley Family, or from the files of the Minnesota Legionnaire.

THE LAST OF THE FOUNDERS

George Washington Bentley was counting the days in Paris, waiting to go home after the conclusion of the First World War, when he saw an ad in the Stars and Stripes newspaper about a meeting to discuss the forming of a post-war soldier's organization. Bentley attended the caucus, and 80 years later this Minnesotan survived to become the last living founder of The American Legion.

In the late 1980s, George Washington Bentley was asked by a reporter if he had any specific goals left in his long life.

"Yes," he replied. "I'd like to be the last living founder of The American Legion. And, you know I'm 90 and so I think I've got a pretty good shot at it."

In 1997, Bentley reached that goal. He became the last man in the most prestigious last man's club of The American Legion.

He was the only survivor of the 2,500 or so veterans who gathered either at the Paris, France, or St. Louis, Missouri, caucuses in 1919 where the nation's largest veteran's organization was founded.

Having survived to reach that goal, he was asked about what other things he'd like to achieve in his long and productive life.

"I'd like to live at least until the year 2000," he said. "That way I'll have lived in three different centuries." Bentley came close, but did not quite accomplish that last goal. He died June 4, 1999, at the Minneapolis VA Medical Center.

George Washington Bentley was born in Montgomery, Minnesota, on February 19, 1898.

The proximity of his birthday to that of another great American founder's prompted his parents to name him after America's first President.

He was the third out of nine children born to Frank and Anna Bentley. Frank was a barber and a standout amateur baseball player who had spent three years trying his hand at the Alaskan gold rush. His luck had never quite panned out in Alaska and he returned to Minnesota to pursue other careers.

Anna had emigrated from Czechoslovakia as a child. The two had been married in Minneapolis in 1894.

George Bentley was a good student at Sherman High School in Montgomery, and he participated in many of the athletics the school offered.

After graduation in 1916, he worked at various manual labor jobs including working in the farm fields for five cents an hour or doing cement work for 10 hours a day for 15 cents an hour.

America entered the Great War in 1917, but Bentley said that it took a while for the war fever to work its way down to Montgomery. One day in 1918, Bentley and four friends decided it was time to enlist in the U.S. Army to fight for their country.

"There wasn't much action in Montgomery."

They rode the train up to Minneapolis and told the recruiter they were interested in joining the part of the Army that would get them overseas the quickest. They were told that the "Engineers" was the best way to get into the action.

A touch of the flu that was epidemic in America that year kept Bentley at home while his friends reported to duty in Minneapolis. Bentley arrived a few days late, "and I never caught up with them."

Bentley was first sent to Jefferson Barracks in St. Louis where he got his shots and clothing. "I'm only 5'7", and I really felt like the little country boy from Minnesota." After about 10 days, the recruits did more training at Washington Barracks in the nation's capital. It was in Washington that Bentley found out that one of the primary weapons of an engineer was a number two shovel.

The unit marched at night from Washington to a port in New Jersey where they boarded a French ship. "I suppose they did everything at night so that spies wouldn't know the movements of the troops."

Bentley's unit left from New Jersey on the SS Dante Allegheri, part of a 12-ship convoy protected by destroyers. Fourteen days and one sub scare later, the ship unloaded the soldiers at Brest, France.

The doughboys spent a great deal of time drilling at Angiers, and then were shipped off to the front if they were judged to be in good health and shape. Bentley, however, drew a different kind of duty. He was sent to Paris and assigned the job of watching over war materials that were sent to France and making sure they got to the front.

"I wasn't really in the action myself, and that was okay with me. If I'd seen more action, I might not be here talking with you today."

Pay for the privates was $30 with a $3 bonus for serving overseas. "But $15 went home on my allotment and $6 went for insurance. All we had to spend for the month was $12."

< GEORGE WASHINGTON BENTLEY
in uniform in 1918 during World War I.

> SALUTING THE TROOPS
Bentley lived his final years at the Minnesota Masonic Home in Bloomington.

THE GYMNASTICS TEAM

at Sherman High School in Montgomery in 1914 featured an aspiring gymnast at the far right. Bentley was active in several school athletic programs.

1914   MONTGOMERY SOKOLS (GYMNASTS)
FRANK Pribyl
STANDING L-R   JIM LINBERGER, BILL KROCAK, HENRY KALINA, EMIL KROCAK
C-Ro (Kaiwer,
HENRY TRCKA, GEORGE BENTLEY   \   FELIX HRUBY
SITTING L-R   ED.DEJCMAR, FRANK SOERS, EMIL STEPANEK, FRANK BUSTA
HENRY TRCKA

Bentley's job entailed being handed a stack of lading bills when the material was loaded on a train at a French port, and then staying with the material until it was unloaded at its destination in France, often close to where the fighting was going on. "My job was just to make sure it got there, I suppose."

Bentley was issued two wool blankets and told to stay with the material no matter what. It usually meant sleeping on the open flatcars for two or three nights, "and it was getting awfully cold at night in September."

One night, Bentley slipped away from his train and checked into a nearby hotel for the night. To his horror, when he returned to the trainyard in the morning, his shipment had departed without him. Always resourceful, he boarded a passenger train - without a ticket - and waved his bills of lading at the conductor.

Since neither spoke the other's language, it took a while to communicate what was going on. Bentley had to transfer to another passenger train before he finally caught up with his shipment.

Once, his duties took him close to the fighting in the St. Mihel sector. The roar of the anti-aircraft fire through the night convinced him that his supply duties were better than being at the front. The area was dark, and Bentley asked where the lights were.

One of the soldiers answered, "In the morning, we're going over the top, and we don't want to let the enemy know what's going on." The major St. Mihel offensive began the next day.

The Germans were lofting shells into Paris at the time Bentley was stationed there. "They were trying to hit the Eiffel Tower or the Notre Dame Cathedral, but they never hit either one. The shells would land with a lot of noise and smoke, but they didn't do much damage."

When the war ended on November 11th, 1918, Bentley was re-assigned to the information desk at Headquarters in Paris. On three-day passes, he and other soldiers were able to travel by train to the sites of the major battles of the war. While there, they were able to see the horrors and oddities of the war, including one area where everything -- woods, bushes, tall grass -- was cut down at a two-foot height by the machine gun fire.

Bentley and the others also were able to rummage through the battlegrounds for souvenirs, and the young lad from Minnesota was able to take home German helmets, clothing, and a sharpshooter's rifle. The items are still in the family.

Time passed slowly for the troops waiting to be sent home. "After the armistice, the morale of the soldiers fell apart," Bentley said. "They felt their job was finished, and they wanted to return to the States as soon as possible."

In March, 1919, Bentley saw a notice in the Stars and Stripes, the official newspaper of the American Expeditionary Force, that there would be a meeting to discuss the establishment of a post-war organization. The group forming the Legion had also advertised in the Paris edition of the New York Herald.

"We went more or less out of curiosity. We were always looking for something to do. Most of the people who came were officers. They were the only ones who could get leave and could afford to get there."

Bentley said that many of the officers were assigned to attend the meeting. Others were motivated to create an organization similar to the Grand Army of the Republic that emerged from the Civil War, and others were just hungry to pass the time. "The soldiers were bored. They were waiting to go home."

The three-day meeting was held at the Cirque de Paris, an old theater that was being used by an American aid association.

Lt. Col. Theodore Roosevelt Jr., the son of the president

> THE PARIS CAUCUS of 1919 marked the beginning of the American Legion. Several hundred American soldiers gathered in Paris to make plans for a post-war organization. George Washington Bentley, who was not an official delegate to the caucus, sat in the balcony section.

and one of the handful of American officers who first conceived of the notion of a post-war organization, was not at the Paris Caucus, Bentley said. He had been shipped home just before it began.

Bentley, who was neither an officer nor one who represented a regiment or other unit, spent his time in the balcony as the participants below debated the issues about forming The American Legion. "It was just like a political rally.

"Everything they were doing seemed kind of vague." In the end, the group decided to meet again in the United States in six weeks at St. Louis.

"There were lots of speeches and lots of debates. We didn't know what we were creating exactly, but we knew that veterans and families needed to recover from the war. The American Legion was the solution to the problems. I was sold on it, there's no doubt about it."

Nobody knows for sure how many people attended the Paris Caucus. It was at least 400 and it could have been quite a few more.

"A lot of the guys were AWOL in Paris, and they didn't want to sign their names," Bentley said. "I was one of those who did sign my name."

Bentley was finally shipped home in October of 1919. He returned to Minneapolis where he sold encyclopedias door to door as he courted his future wife, Alma Pretoria Crane. She had been born in England.

The day after Christmas in 1920, the couple devised a scheme to elope. They told Alma's mother that they were simply "going for a walk date."

Alma's little sister, Babe, wanted to go along, however, and though the couple wanted desperately to be alone, the mother informed them, "If you don't take your sister, you don't go at all."

The three of them hopped a series of streetcars that took them to the Lake of the Isles area of Minneapolis where Bentley's cousin, a minister, lived. He pronounced the solemn vows for the couple.

Babe, who was nine, simply thought the minister was practicing doing a wedding, but on the way home in the streetcar with the newlyweds she figured out what had happened.

Any hopes that the Bentleys had of keeping their secret went out the window when Babe burst into the house ahead of the couple and announced, "They're married. They're married!"

Bentley's mother-in-law, who was clearing the table at the time, took one look at George and whopped him on the head with a large serving tray.

"She was unhappy we hadn't told her," he said. "Later we became good friends."

The marriage lasted 65 years and produced one offspring. George's son served in the U.S. Army Air Corps from 1945-47, and his grandson, Frank, served in the First Air Cavalry in Vietnam.

George worked at the U.S. Post Office from 1920 until 1963. When he could get away, he went up to northern Minnesota for hunting and fishing, and even as he reached the century mark, his eyes would still light up when he talked about the big buck he shot or the stringers of fish he used to catch.

He joined the organization he helped create in 1922 at the Calhoun Post in Minneapolis, and he is a life member there. On special occasions, he still proudly wears his Legion cap and the medal that was awarded him as a founder.

In 1981, Bentley was elected president of the Society of American Legion Founders Ltd., a group that had already shrunk to about 50 members by then. Bentley's card shows him to be member number 40.

He attended and spoke at several national conventions, and he was able to drive his car until age 94.

To the end, Bentley was proud of his small part in history. "The Legion has been my life. We never thought it would become so large. But it's an organization that serves everybody and everything. The United States of America will be kept on an even keel under the watchful eye of The American Legion."

This story was assembled using various newspaper interviews through the years, and an interview with Bentley by the Minnesota Legionnaire in 1998.

GREAT WAR HAD ITS OWN SLANG

Ammos -- Standard issue boots

Archie -- Anti-aircraft fire

Banjo -- Aussie for shovel

Barker -- Sausage (thinking they were made of dog meat)

Bonk, to -- Shell with artillery fire

Bonzer -- Good, cool

Bung -- Cheese

Buzzer -- Field Telephone

Chub -- Shut up!

Conchie -- Conscientious Objector

Crump -- Shell burst

Dixie -- Food container

Duck board -- Boards used to line the bottoms of trenches

Egg -- Hand grenade

Emma Gee -- Machine Gun

Ersatz -- German reserves

Fritz -- German

Heinie -- German

Hop the Bags -- Going over the top

Maconochie -- Canned stew

Napoo -- Done, used up

Phutt -- To stop functioning

Provo -- Military Police

Ragtime -- Disorderly, absurd

Sammy -- American soldier

Stunt -- Attack or Raid

Uncle Charlie -- Full marching orders

BENTLEY'S DIARY CHRONICLES HIS DUTY IN FRANCE IN 1918

Editor's Note: George Washington Bentley enlisted in the U.S. Army in 1918.

On June 14, 1918, Bentley left on a troop ship for France, and he arrived on June 27 at Brest, France. Bentley began keeping a diary a few days before he joined the Army and kept it through his time in France. His entries are short and to the point.

These selections from his diary cover from the time he landed in France until Armistice Day, Nov. 11, 1918.

JUNE

Friday, June 28 — Disembark at 12.00 oclock. March to Fontanazen Barracks.

29 — This place is where Napoleon had his troops.

30 — Place where they hung and shot people is still here. See the wall with lots of holes in it.

JULY

3 — Have a ball game (in the) afternoon. We win. Wash clothes today also.

5 — Packing to leave barracks. Take French train to Angers. Hard riding.

6 — Arrive at Angers at 10:30 A.M. Large barracks built by Germans.

7 — Have two wine houses here. Stephen and I have a bottle together.

8 — Our first drill day. Take a bath, sign cards. Get a speech from a lieutenant.

9 — Drill, drill, drill. (In) cadence. Band concert this night. Soldier gives us a dance.

10 — Drill, drill, drill. Regimental parade. Go downtown by river. 4,000 troops.

11 — Drill, drill, drill. Five American ladies give program at night. Outside stage.

16 — Gas mask drill. Speech by an Englishman at Angers University Club.

18 — Drill, drill, drill. Boxing tonight. I put on gloves.

19 — Rifle range. First 10 shots, make nine bull's eyes. Last five, I make four bull's eyes.

22 — Gas drill. Go through chamber. Mask is OK.

23 — Wire entanglements. Have charge of detail. Put up wires and take them down.

25 — Trench digging & dugouts. Transferred to Co. G.

26 — Back to Co. L. Rifle range afternoon. Set at 500 yds. Not so good as before.

30 — I get orders to go to Paris. Transferred to Co. C. Get pass until 11 p.m.

31 — Pack up, get ready to leave. Leave Angers for Paris at 3.

AUGUST

Thursday, August 1 — Arrive Paris 7.00 oclock. Eat at Palace Hotel. Room at Alexandria Hotel.

2 — Go down to the warehouse. Ride around in trucks. Eat at the Mediterranee.

5 — Long range gun shots to bombard Paris. It never does much damage anyway.

6 — Big Bertha again starts to shoot. Some people are killed.

7 — Get orders to go on a convoy. Leave in afternoon at 5.30. To Bourges France.

9 — In Versailles this morning. (   ) afternoon. Go back to Paris at night.

15 — Report at Lieut. Booth's Office. Pay day for two months. Take in the YMCA downtown in Paris.

16 — Still down at the warehouse. Nothing to do so we 3 play cards to pass the time away.

22 — Arrive Paris early morning. Another convoy to Bourges. 2 bath tubs and six sinks.

27 — Report this morning. Turned over to Gen. Purch. Agent 10 boxes tools for La Rochelle. Leave tonight at 11.20 p.m.

28 — Arrive Tours. 5.00 a.m. Stay all day. Take in the town. Stay near the station.

29 — Car goes out early this morning. I go out at noon. Stop at Niort overnight. Car not located.

30 — Eat at Engr's mess hall in one of the buildings. Leave afternoon for LaRochelle. Stay in first class coach.

31 — Still no sign of the car. Take in the town. Leave tonight for Samur.

SEPTEMBER

Sunday, September 1 — Arrive this morning at Samur. Stay here till one oclock. Car not located. Leave and arrive at Niort.

2 — Stay at Niort today until 4 p.m. Leave for La Rochelle. Shipment arrives. Eat at 31st messhall.

8 — Rain today. Go down to warehouse. Play game. Play at hotel. Big show at YMCA.

9— Nothing doing today. Issue of tobacco. Rain tonight. Can't go out. Stay around hotel.

10 — Blue print paper brought down to warehouse. Filled up one of the rooms. One of my blankets stolen.

11 — Report at Palace Elysee. Receive three checks. Cashed at Room 211 Place Elysee Hotel.

15 — Two big air raids by the Boche. One at 1.30 a.m. and 4 a.m. Quite a lot of damage done in Paris.

21— Stick around warehouse today. Receive my check for last trip. Spend all of it too.

23 — Orders to convoy a water tank to Bordeaux. Hard job finding car in yards. Leave for Bordeaux.

24 — Wake up this morning in Juvisy. Eat at cantina. Leave afternoon. Big aviation camp here. Lots of airplanes.

OCTOBER

Tuesday, Oct. 1 — Washday for me. Trip to commissary. Palais Hotel YMCA. Write five letters.

4 — Traveling orders to go to Allerly with a car of sinks. Leave Gare de Lyon at 11.30 p.m.

6 — Arrive Allerey. Deliver convoy. Eat at Hosp. 25. Meet J.L. Keohn from my old hometown. Oh joy!

7 — Leave at 9 a.m. for Paris. Change to Chalon. wait at Dyon for an hour. Arrive Paris 8.00 p.m. No supper. Oh, joy.

17 — English Theatre. Play named Zig Zag. Lot of fun. Good show. Good theatre. Received checks. 85 frs.

20 — Big celebration. Class of 1920 called out. Aeroplanes, machine guns, artillery, shell balloons on exhibition at Concorde.

22 — Leave for Nancy. Pass through Chateau Thierry. Many shell holes, dugouts, cannons and graves along the tracks. Foul sector.

23 — Sleep at YMCA. Take a trolley out to Pompey. See two Hun aeroplanes shot down. Hear the roar of guns at the front. Leave Pompey tonight.

26 — Leave Vitry arrive Hausson. Eat & sleep with ordinance car left in yard. Take in YMCA show. Lots of big guns here mounted on railway cars. Camouflaged. Someone steals two pairs of my shoes.

NOVEMBER

Friday, Nov. 1, 1918 — Turn in orders. French holiday today. No one works.

3 — Palais de Glace. Today take in (   ) there. Date tonight with a real nice madmoiselle.

5 — On the job again. No breakfast. Slept too late. Big boxing tournament at Palais de Glace. Lots of fuss.

7 — Still raining. Many accidents. Stay in tonight and take a good long and refreshing bath. Oh lala.

8 — Date tonight. La la. Rumors of peace. People all excited. YMCA ce soir.

9 — Germany given 72 hours to sign armistice. Place de la Concorde ce soir.

10 — Play games afternoon. Come out ahead. Go to 133 Rd. St. Michel tonight. She left at 7.00 p.m. Missed her.

11 — Armistice signed at 11 a.m. this morning. Bells ring. Guns shot off. Flags up. Great excitement. Celebrate tonight.

12— Holiday today. Streets are packed. Cannon dragged around the streets. Band playing. Stay out till 2.00 a.m. Very tired.

13 — More celebration. Yanks celebrate tonight. Meet at the Place de la Opera. Lots of fun. Get in at 3.00 a.m.

14 — Sore throat this morning from yelling so much. Take treatment. Stay in tonight. Take bath. Go to bed.

MEDAL OF HONOR RECIPIENT

Mike Colalillo of Duluth was in Washington D.C. recently for a reunion of Medal of Honor recipients.

All photos are from the personal collection of Mike Colalillo.

THE MEDAL OF HONOR

Growing up on the tough streets of West Duluth, 19-year-old Mike Colalillo had no notion of getting any medals when he became a one-man spearhead for his company in a battlefield in Germany during World War II. Later, when President Truman pinned the Medal of Honor on Colalillo's uniform, he told him, 'I'd rather have one of these than be president.'

Editor's Note: The underlined sections below are excerpts from Mike Colalillo's citation for the Medal of Honor.

Entered service at Duluth, Minn. Birth: Hibbing, Minn.

Carlo Colalillo emigrated from Italy in the early 1920s and settled in the Town of Stuntz, just outside Hibbing. He worked in the iron mines.

As time went by, he saved enough money to bring his wife, Vittoria, and four children over, and they joined him in Hibbing. On December 1, 1925, a son was born to the Colalillos, and they named him Michael.

Eventually the family grew to nine children, and Carlo moved to Duluth where he got a job at a plant that made carbon for batteries. Later, he got a better job at the Inter-Lake Iron Co. in West Duluth.

Mike Colalillo grew up on Raleigh Street, a tough neighborhood by any standards.

"We were all in trouble at one time or another. Everybody got in trouble. I suppose I did too."

The Colalillo's house was right next to the railroad tracks, and a major occupation for the boys in the neighborhood was to climb aboard the cars and throw coal to their comrades below. The coal could then be sold or used to heat the local homes.

When Mike was 16, his mother died, leaving his father with four children still at home.

"I said, 'Dad, I want to quit school.' I felt I had to help take care of the family. He didn't like it very much, but I did it anyway."

Mike got a job at the Grand Bakery on 57th Avenue West as a baker's helper. "I did everything from cleaning the pans to putting jelly in the bismarcks."

Not long after Michael Colalillo turned 18, he was drafted. It was 1944, and the war had been going on for several years. "We all knew we had to go. There was nobody around anymore, so I didn't mind it that much."

He took his physical at Ft. Snelling, and then a few days later boarded a train for Camp Fanning, Texas, for basic training.

Rank and organization: Private First Class, U.S. Army, 2nd Squad, 2nd Platoon, Company C, 1st

another machine gun emplacement and silenced all resistance in his area, killing at least three and wounding an
undetermined number of riflemen as they fled.

The tank rolled on, occasionally firing its cannon.
"Could I feel it? I was right on top of the turret. Boy,
could I feel it."

"The tank captain would say off to the right or off to the
left. I was a rifleman, but in basic they train you on all the
weapons. And when guys want to take a nap on the front
lines, you'd man their machine guns for a while. I knew
how to use it."

At a critical juncture, the machine gun jammed, though,
and great effort by Colalillo would not make it work again.

His machine gun eventually jammed; so he secured a sub-
machine gun from the tank crew to continue his attack on
foot.

Collalillo got the attention of the tank captain. "I told
the guy in the tank that the machine gun had
jammed. He said, 'Here, take our Thompson.' He gave me
some ammo, and told me to be careful getting off the
tank."

Colalillo advanced on foot, firing the Thompson as he
went. The tanks, however, had run out of ammunition by
this time, and were ordered to the rear. Colalillo's unit was
also ordered to fall back.

When our armored forces exhausted their ammunition and
the order to withdraw was given, he remained behind to
help a seriously wounded comrade over several hundred
yards of open terrain rocked by an intense enemy artillery
and mortar barrage.

Colalillo also was withdrawing from the area, but then
he stopped. "I heard a voice say, 'Mike, Mike, I'm hit.'
So I helped him back to our lines. We could hear other
guys crying out there, but they wouldn't let us go get them.
They thought maybe they were Germans trying to trick us
into going out. But in the morning we did go out and
picked up two guys. They were still alive."

After another day's fighting, the division captured the town
and then was immediately relieved and spent three or four

days behind the lines.

After the rest, the 100th Division was ordered back on the
front lines. As they were getting ready to move out,
Colalillo's unit was approached by a platoon runner who
had two MPs with him.

They had orders to escort Colalillo back to headquarters. "I
told them I didn't do a God darn thing, and I didn't need to
have any MPs take me back."

When he was brought to headquarters, he was informed
that he had been nominated by the tank captain for the
Medal of Honor. Colalillo's reaction was basically the same
as when he was informed about the Silver Star. "I said,
'What the hell's a Medal of Honor?' They had to explain to
me what it meant. I said, 'But what the hell did I do?' I
really didn't remember all of it, but the tank guy had
explained most of it to them."

He was sent to Paris for a few days, and then on to
Washington D.C. In an interview with the military brass, he
was asked if he wanted to stay in the service or get out.

"I told them I wanted to go home."

He was sent to Camp McCoy in Wisconsin to be processed
out of the military. "I was in a room with a bunch of other
guys, and I just sat there like a bump on a log and they
never called out my name. Finally I was the last one left in
the room, and the clerk said, 'Where's this guy supposed
to go?'"

After looking at his papers, the clerk discovered he had a
Medal of Honor recipient in front of him. He quickly got the
colonel, and Colalillo got his own room at the camp.

The next day, he had to go through various medical tests
and dental checkups, and that evening Colalillo headed for
the PX for a beer. There he ran into an old friend from his
neighborhood in West Duluth, Louie Shumich.

After Shumich found out that Colalillo had earned the
Medal of Honor, he became his escort for the rest of the
trip home. "There was a bar on the train, and even though
I was only 19 years old, they were serving us. I never had
to buy a drink."

Already well lubricated, the two got a bottle of liquor before
they boarded the bus to Duluth in Minneapolis. "Everybody
on the bus was drinking, and we were passing that bottle
around."

When the bus pulled into the West Duluth station, a small
group of well wishers and family were gathered to greet
the new hero. Members of Shumich's family were also

PRESIDENT TRUMAN

presented Colalillo with the Medal of Honor in a ceremony at the White House and told him that he rather have the medal than be president.

< A GROUP PHOTO

was taken at the White House following the presentations by President Harry S Truman.

>THE BACK OF THE MEDAL

tells the name of the recipient, the branch of service, the place the medal was earned and the date of the action.

there. The trouble was that nobody got off the bus.

"They went up to the bus driver and told him that a couple of guys were supposed to get off at this stop. They went to the back of the bus and found us passed out. They woke us up so we could get off the bus."

Colalillo was feted by the VFW and the American Legion and other organizations for a period, and then it was time to travel to Washington D.C. to receive his medal. He was accompanied by his dad, his brother and his brother's wife, and two sisters.

"They put us up at a big hotel, and we all had rooms. It was the best time we'd ever had. A captain was assigned to us, and he took us around to every place. Nothing was cheap, and we were at clubs and we went dancing. My dad said, 'Who's going to pay for all this,' and they told him, 'The government.'"

Colalillo went to the Pentagon and then, on December 18, 1945, he and his entourage went to the White House to receive the medal. "There were six or seven of us, and they searched us pretty good."

Gen. Dwight Eisenhower was in attendance at the presentation.

By his intrepidity and inspiring courage Pfc. Colalillo gave tremendous impetus to his company's attack, killed or wounded 25 of the enemy in bitter fighting, and assisted a wounded soldier in reaching the American lines at great risk of his own life.

As the fifth man out of six to receive the medal that day, Colalillo patiently waited his turn, and when President Harry S Truman hung the medal over his head, the president said to him, "I'm proud of you. I rather have this than be president."

He remembers the look on his dad's face when he got the medal. "He was pretty calm, but his eyes popped out when he got to shake hands with the president."

Colalillo returned home to Duluth, and a month later he was honored in a city-wide celebration in his honor that featured the governor as the main speaker. At about that time he also received the Silver Star and a Bronze Star for his earlier heroics.

Afterwards, he tried college for a time and played some college football. He later got a job at Inter-Lake Iron where his father worked. His father died the following year.

The hell of combat stayed with Colalillo in the coming years. "I adjusted pretty well. I had a few nightmares, and when a car would backfire, I'd jump, but as time goes by it all fades away."

He married Lina in 1946, and continued to work at the

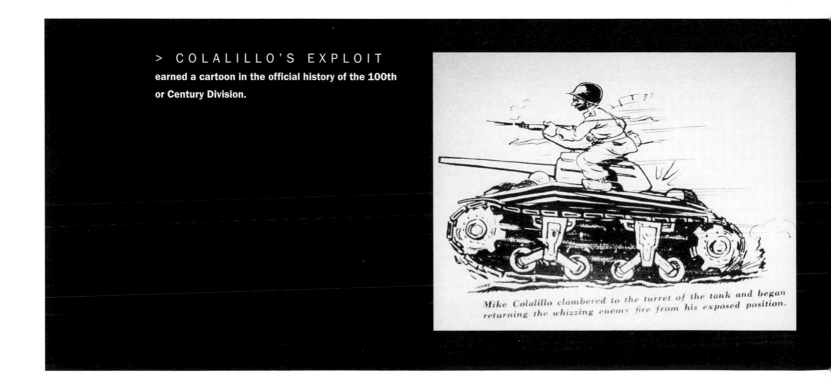

> COLALILLO'S EXPLOIT
earned a cartoon in the official history of the 100th or Century Division.

Mike Colalillo clambered to the turret of the tank and began returning the whizzing enemy fire from his exposed position.

iron plant. They had three children. He suffered a serious injury when he got his arm caught in a conveyor at the iron plant, and he lost much of the use of the arm. When the plant closed in 1959, he was out of work.

"I was fortunate that my brother was president of the long-shoremen, and he got me into the union. That's just when the seaway was opening up, and the port of Duluth was booming. I worked there for 29 years, the last 19 as foreman at the warehouse."

Colalillo retired in 1987, and that same year had a triple bypass heart surgery. The surgery has held up, but he is on a strict regimen of medications.

Did he ever get job offers along the way based on his Medal of Honor? "Yeah, I had offers, but they were always looking for a talker, and I'm not a talker. What I should have done is stayed in the service. I would have had it made."

He gets mail constantly from people around the country, some just to congratulate him, and others who are seeking autographs. He always writes back.

Looking back on being one of a handful who received the nation's highest honor, Colalillo is characteristically humble.

"If that officer hadn't been there to see it, it would never have happened. Others did the same thing I did, but there was nobody there to see the action.

"I happened to be in the right place at the right time."

PRESIDENT KENNEDY
greeted Colalillo during a reunion of Medal of Honor recipients at the White House in the early 60s.

All photos from Frank Kinney's personal collection.

A TALE OF TWO SHIPS

In the course of World War II, there were some sailors who survived the sinking of their ship and lived to tell about it. Frank Kinney of Chatfield lived to tell about two of them. Aboard both the USS Wasp and the USS Princeton, aircraft carriers serving in the south Pacific, Kinney followed the order to abandon ship after Japanese attacks. In all, Kinney served aboard four ships in his naval career.

His nickname probably never was "Lucky." Frank Kinney served on four ships before and during World War II, and two of them were sunk.

Twice Kinney was on the crew of an aircraft carrier in a battle against the Japanese. Twice he found himself in the drink in the South Pacific. Twice he was rescued and was able to serve his country again.

Kinney, who has lived in Minnesota since 1964, grew up in Ayer, Massachusetts. When he was still in high school he saw a recruiting poster that proclaimed "Earn, Learn and Travel," and he traveled to Boston in March 1938 to enlist in the U.S. Navy.

Kinney's father had died when he was five, and his mother had taught school to keep the family together. "You didn't have fun in those days, you worked." After high school, Kinney worked on a farm until he was finally called up by the Navy in October of 1938.

He was excited about joining up. "I had the travel uppermost in my mind," said Kinney, who lives in Chatfield in southeastern Minnesota. "And nobody talked about war in those days. Nobody."

After bootcamp in Newport, Rhode Island, Kinney was given orders to the heavy cruiser Wichita, and he spent a year aboard. At first, his role on the ship was deck hand, but he tired of scrubbing the decks and shining the bright work.

He was convinced by shipmates to join the engineers. "I really wanted to apprentice in the bake shop, but I could see that wasn't going to happen."

Kinney was assigned to the boiler room where he began his apprenticeship as a machinist's mate. During his first year, he worked his way up from apprentice seaman ($21 a month) to seaman second class ($36 a month) to Seaman First Class ($54 a month).

He was transferred to the USS Wasp as the new carrier was readied for her maiden voyage. Assigned to the "A" Division, he eventually was given the job of running the hydraulics for the massive aircraft elevators that ran between the hangar deck and the flight deck. His duty station was five decks below the hangar deck in the bowels of the ship.

The Wasp was tied up in Bermuda when news of Pearl Harbor came. "That was some pretty good liberty, but I'll tell you, we didn't stay in Bermuda very long."

Again Kinney and his mates took the trip through the Panama Canal. "On one of those trips through the canal, I was out on liberty and I couldn't find the ship when I got back. Too many of those rum and Cokes."

For the next 17 months, the ship seemed to be constantly at sea. "We could go 300 miles a day, and we went 300 miles every day. My feet got so tired of that steel deck, they were just itching for some sand between my toes."

The ship headed for the South Pacific in June of 1943. In December, the Princeton was ordered to the shipyards at Bremerton for some refitting. The men were given ample time to enjoy their stay ashore.

"The only way you could get liquor was to buy it on the black market, usually from the guys who drove the cabs. All you could get was Sunny Brook, and they charged $15 or $16 a bottle. Those cabbies must have gotten rich."

Back in the Pacific, the Princeton followed the U.S. forces island hopping across the Pacific. When the army landed at Leyte Island on the Philippines, the Princeton was supporting the landing with air cover.

Kinney had advanced to first class machinist's mate by this time, and his job was to run the throttle for the forward engines. "There were about 35 gauges on the wall and two throttles. I had the engineering officer standing behind me watching every move I made."

On October 24, 1944, an armor piercing bomb from a Japanese aircraft hit the Princeton's flight deck, slicing through to the hangar deck, and then down into the mess deck below where it exploded. It ignited six torpedo planes on the hangar deck, and the ship was soon engulfed in flames and explosions.

"I thought the end of the world had come. For a moment you just go into shock and you can't do anything. It was the same as the last time, all the lights went out."

Kinney was amazed at the discipline aboard the ship. "One of the reasons the officers carry a pistol is to maintain good order. But I never saw a single man lose it. Everyone did what he was trained to do. It was amazing how calm everyone seemed to be."

The engineers stayed at their station for a half hour as the crew tried to save the ship.

With the order given to abandon ship, again Kinney made his way topside. There were no ropes leading down to the sea, but Kinney grabbed a two inch fuel hose that was draped over the side and lowered himself into the water.

"I wasn't in the water more than 15 or 20 minutes when a destroyer came along." Ropes were hanging down the side of the destroyer, the USS Irwin (DD 794), and he grabbed at one of them. "Myself and another guy grabbed the rope at the same time. The water was going over our heads, and he was even more frantic than I was. He thought he was going to drown. So I let him have the rope, and I tried to grab another."

The destroyer was moving slowly through the water, and Kinney watched nearly the whole rescue ship go by before he was finally able to grab the last rope on the stern. "I was holding on to the rope but the screw (propeller) was sucking me down. It was all I could do to hold onto the rope. Meanwhile, there were about three crew members trying to haul me in. They finally pulled me up like a sack of potatoes. I laid on the deck for 15 minutes trying to catch my breath. I was just full of sea water. I was close to being on the verge of drowning, but I made it."

Meanwhile, the captain of the Princeton was still trying to save his ship. Other Navy ships, including the cruiser Birmingham, came along side with fire hoses pouring water on the Princeton's infernos.

The Birmingham was gaining ground on the fires when she was ordered to back off because of a possible Japanese attack. "The flames came back up then, and when the Birmingham came back with its hoses, the Princeton just blew up. It was one hell of an explosion."

In all, 108 men were killed on the Princeton and 229 were killed on the Birmingham. Kinney took part in the ceremony as the men were buried at sea.

Again, Kinney and the others were transported to Esperito Santos and then back to the United States. Again, he got 30 days leave. Again, he was ordered to Bremerton, Washington.

Kinney spent the remainder of the war in a relatively safe place, aboard the destroyer USS Lawrence, cruising back and forth on patrol outside San Francisco Bay. "With all that stuff going on in 1945, and all those kamikaze attacks, I was glad I was in a safe spot."

Kinney remembers clearly the last day of the war.

"I was in a warehouse in San Francisco getting a pound of sugar with a ration coupon. Just then, you couldn't believe the racket that started up. There were bells and horns and sirens. It was just bedlam.

"The lady behind the counter said, 'What do you know, son. It sounds like the war is over. How would you like another pound of sugar?'"

Kinney went to agricultural college in Washington, and eventually his work for the American Breeder's Association took him to Minnesota where he has lived for the past 37 years.

Through the years he has amassed a collection of books, magazines and photos about the Wasp and Princeton. Kinney, who was cheerful all through the telling of his war experiences, started to choke up as he held a photo of his Class of 1938 at Ayer High School. "There were 23 boys in the class, and these four were killed," he said, silently pointing out the four. Finally, he is able to talk again. "Imagine that. One-sixth of my class was killed in the war."

ON GUARD DUTY

during boot camp in Newport, Rhode Island, in 1938, Kinney shows off his inspection best.

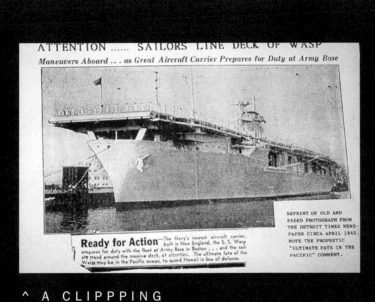

^ A CLIPPING FROM A NEWSPAPER

shows the USS Wasp as it is readied for action in Boston in 1940.

> THE USS PRINCETON

is shown with its full complement of aircraft. The fast carrier was built on the hull of a cruiser.

Avis Dagit Schorer often worked under conditions that were challenging to both the doctors and nurses.

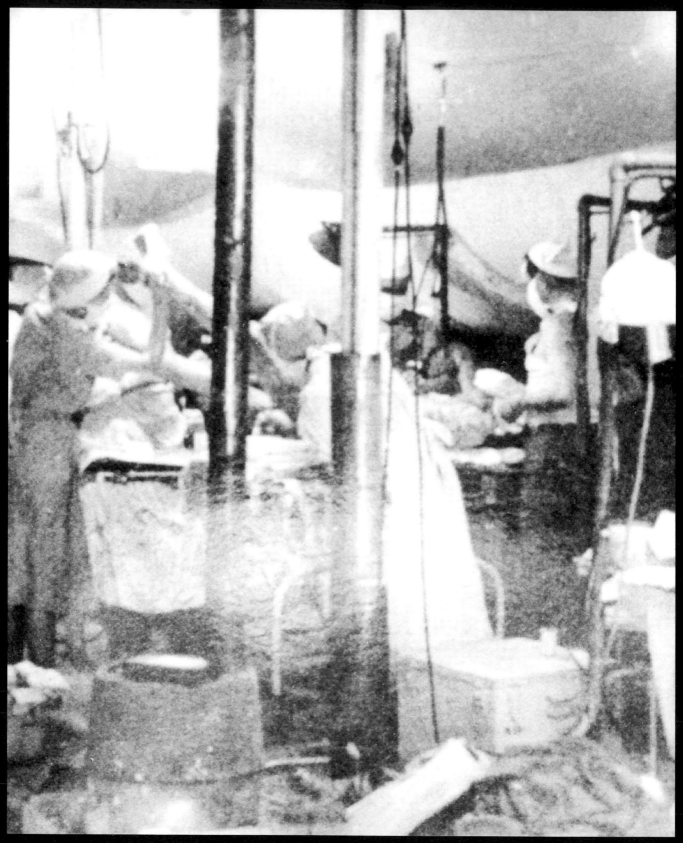

Photos are from the personal collection of Avis Dagit Schorer.

A NURSE RECALLS
HELL'S HALF ACRE

Avis Dagit Schorer grew up on a farm in Iowa, one of eleven children. When war broke out in 1941, she joined the regular Army as a nurse and an officer. In 1944, the 56th Evacuation Hospital was landed at Anzio, one of the bloodiest beachheads of the war. The unit endured 76 days of pounding on a piece of real estate that later became know as 'Hell's Half Acre.'

Avis Dagit Schorer grew up on a farm in Iowa during the Great Depression. She now lives in a spacious apartment in Bloomington. She had a long career in the medical field, and she now spends part of her time as a volunteer at a local library.

She has stayed active in later years, and has even written a book.

There's one thing, though, that separates Schorer from many of her neighbors and fellow library volunteers. She was a combat nurse who lived through some of the toughest times and places of World War II.

Avis Dagit was one of 11 kids who grew up on a Green County, Iowa, farm, and after high school she went away to nurses training at Methodist Hospital in Des Moines. "With all those kids, you can't all stay at home."

After graduating, she signed an agreement with the American Red Cross that she would serve her country if a crisis developed. With Europe already at war, and the world situation deteriorating, that crisis seemed likely.

"I knew on December 7th, 1941, that I was in."

Following the attack on Pearl Harbor, she was given some time to wind up her civilian affairs, and on March 17, 1942 — her birthday— she reported to the U.S. Army in Des Moines. She was immediately sent to Camp Chaffee in Arkansas.

"When we got there, it was nothing but a few scattered buildings and some dirt roads. Not long afterwards, though, the troops started pouring in."

Within a year, the base was home to 100,000 men and it had its own 1,000-bed hospital. "It was unbelievable how quickly it developed." (The camp gained fame in later years as the destination for the Cuban boat people.)

The nurses went through no formal basic training, but simply went to work, learning Army training along the way. "You had to learn as you go. It was a whole new language for me. I'd never heard of a latrine, or a chow line, or a mess hall."

The nurses, who were all commissioned officers, were given strict instructions on not fraternizing with the enlisted men. "But that was easily broken. Some women broke it just to see if they could get away with it."

Second Lieutenant Dagit and her fellow nurses were proud of the fact that they were part of the

"Were we ever glad to see them. They had fresh water and they had food." The men had brought three days of rations with them, but they were getting low.

The paratroopers were relieved from their positions and sent back to the Cherbourg Peninsula to do mop up duty. Then it was back to England to get ready for the next drop, which turned out to be Holland.

Carroll was at Bastogne when it was surrounded by German divisions during the Battle of the Bulge. When the paratroopers were finally reached by Patton's Third Army,

Carroll got a chance to visit with his brother, Jackson, for a couple of hours.

In all, Carroll made 11 jumps in his Army career. His unit was getting ready to head for the Pacific when the war ended.

Carroll moved to Minneapolis after the war and worked as a machinist and machinist supervisor until retirement. At 76, he still works long hours as a charter bus driver, usually taking sports teams to their games.

THE GREATEST INVASION EVER

Almost exactly two and one-half years since the United States had entered World War II, the Allies were poised to launch the greatest invasion force the world had ever seen.

In addition to the action in the Pacific against Japan; the U.S. had fought campaigns in North Africa, Sicily, and Italy as the war had continued through June of 1944.

The fighting had been fierce between the Germans and the Russians through those years, and the Russian leaders had called for a second front in Europe.

The Allies were eager to bring the war to Western Europe, but first the problem of gathering an army, amassing huge quantities of materiel, and somehow getting all that across the English Channel and landing on beaches defended by a determined enemy had to be solved.

Convoy after convoy brought men, tanks, food, clothing, ammunition and millions of tons of other supplies to the United Kingdom where it had to be staged for delivery to France. A huge armada of ships and boats was assembled.

Weather became a problem, and against the advice of some of his staff, Eisenhower decided to press ahead with the attack on June 6, 1944.

British, Canadian and U.S. paratroopers took off on June 5th and were dropped to establish positions behind the German defenses. They were to prevent re-enforcements, smash communications, and, it was hoped, to slow down the German retreat.

The invasion was aimed at a 50-mile stretch of beach in Normandy and involved the U.S. First Army and the British Second Army. The Americans landed on two beaches code named Utah and Omaha. The British, Canadian and other forces landed on Gold, Sword and Juno beaches.

After a naval and air bombardment of the beach defenses, the landing craft made their way to shore. As the men hit the beaches, they were often met by a murderous rain of fire from the cliff positions of the enemy.

Sword, Juno, Gold and Utah were lightly defended and though the Germans put up fierce resistance, the troops were all ashore by afternoon.

Omaha was a different story. Mortars, rockets and machine gun fire poured down from the 150 foot cliffs. The men that got through the water faced barbed wire and metal beams blocking their way.

Through heroic action, the men at Omaha pressed ahead and captured the high positions. Over 155,000 men were ashore at Normandy, and the push to liberate France was on.

By the end of the week 300,000 Allies were landed. By the end of July over 1.4 million troops were in France.

'DEATH WAS ALL AROUND. PEOPLE WERE PRAYING, SCREAMING, CRYING AND CURSING'

First Lieutenant LeRoy Shultz was a tank platoon commander on June 6, 1944. His unit boarded landing tank transports at Southampton about three in the morning and hunkered down for the 160-mile ride through the choppy English Channel to Omaha Beach.

Both seasickness and fear were the order of the day, Shultz recalled.

"There were no atheists aboard those landing craft."

Shultz had been one of the few drafted before the war began. He grew up in Monticello and was working for a trucking business in Minneapolis in May of 1941 "when my uncle with the fuzzy whiskers pointed at me and said, 'I want you.' I had just bought a new car and it wasn't paid for. I had to get rid of that in a hurry."

Shultz was inducted at Ft. Snelling and soon found himself in basic training at Ft. Leonard Wood, Mo. There was more training at Camp Livingston in Louisiana and at Ft. Bragg in North Carolina as 1941 wound down.

"We were heading back to Ft. Livingston in a big convoy and we were the last truck in the line. A car was stopped beside the road and the driver shouted at us, 'Have you heard the news? The Japs have bombed Pearl Harbor.'

"Well, that blew our Christmas furloughs we were all

planning on."

Shultz went to tank training at Camp Young in California, but was picked out of the crowd for his leadership qualities. "I always tell people that they decided they couldn't make a soldier out of me so they sent me to OCS."

He came out as a second lieutenant in April of 1943 and went back to California for more tank training. "One day, they blew the whistle, and we went overseas."

The crossing in a troop ship, the B.B. Alexander, took three weeks. A ship just ahead of the Alexander, the USS Dorchester, was sunk by torpedoes in that convoy. The famous Four Chaplains story came from the Dorchester.

Shultz's unit helped deliver the tanks that were arriving in huge quantities to the various staging areas in southern England. Everyone knew the invasion was coming soon, and the troops waited for the word.

"It rained every day at the beginning of June, and the element of surprise was getting away from us. On the night of the 5th, they said, 'Let's go.' From then on it's kind of a blur to me."

The LVTs were loaded up with three or four tanks per landing craft. The trip was long and rough in the choppy channel and it wasn't until D-Day was well underway that the tank transports came in on the left side of the beach.

"We knew we were getting close to something when we could hear the Navy guns firing toward shore."

The front of the landing craft dropped down, and Shultz led his unit ashore in a jeep that had been made water

FACTS ABOUT D-DAY

-- Over 10,000 Allied troops including 6,000 Americans were killed in the D-Day invasion.

-- Six million tons of supplies were stockpiled in England before the invasion.

-- 155,000 Allies landed the first day.

-- By nightfall, the Allies controlled an area of about 80 square miles of northern France.

-- There were over 5,000 ships involved in the landings.

-- Aboard the ships, the men who weren't seasick enjoyed a pre-invasion feast that included roast beef, steak, chicken, peas, plum pudding and ice cream.

-- The run from the troop ships to the beach in the landing craft was about 8-11 miles.

-- The Allies landed along a stretch of beach 59-miles long.

tight. "I remember the water was over the top of the wheels. It was about up to my waist as we drove in."

The beach was in chaos. "I saw a space and took it. I motioned for everybody else to come ahead. It was sad, confused, hectic -- death was all around. People were screaming, praying, crying and cursing."

Bodies floated in the water, and there were more bodies on the beach. "The infantry boys who landed ahead of us didn't fare very well. Many of them never made it out of the water." Mortar shells exploded all around, but none hit any of the heavy equipment in Shultz's platoon.

The tank company Shultz served in laid low for a while until the fighting moved to the open ground beyond the cliffs where a tank would be of more value. He was involved with the fighting around St. Lo and other places as the U.S. Army headed inland.

A few months later, Shultz was able to ride with his platoon through Paris after it was liberated. He spent much of the rest of the war in action in Belgium and fought in the Battle of the Bulge.

Shultz was in the Third Army commanded by Gen. George Patton. "I only saw him once but that was in California. He was respected for what he could do, but I can tell you that the junior officers thoroughly hated him."

One of the reasons was that Patton required his men to run a mile in the morning with full packs: "And if you didn't make it in the morning, you got to do it in the afternoon. Oh, well, when you're 23 years old, it doesn't bother you that much."

During the course of the war, Shultz saw plenty of action, none of which he really wants to talk about. Along the way, he earned the Silver Star. "They should have a truckload of Silver Stars for all the fellows who were over there."

And he did step on a land mine. "Yes, I've got a few dimples to show I was over there."

And he hasn't seen the movie "Saving Private Ryan" and he doesn't intend to. "But I can tell you from the little snippets I saw on TV that there's one glaring error in that movie. An officer would never wear his captain's bar on his helmet if he was going into combat. The Germans had great respect for leaders, and they liked to shoot ours if they could."

After the war, Shultz stayed in the Army Reserve for a time, and made his career in heavy truck sales. He is retired and lives in Crystal.

< LeROY SHULTZ

was drafted into the army before the war started, but was soon sent to Officer Candidate School.

> DURING THE WAR

Shultz was an officer in a tank unit. After the war he made his career in heavy truck sales.

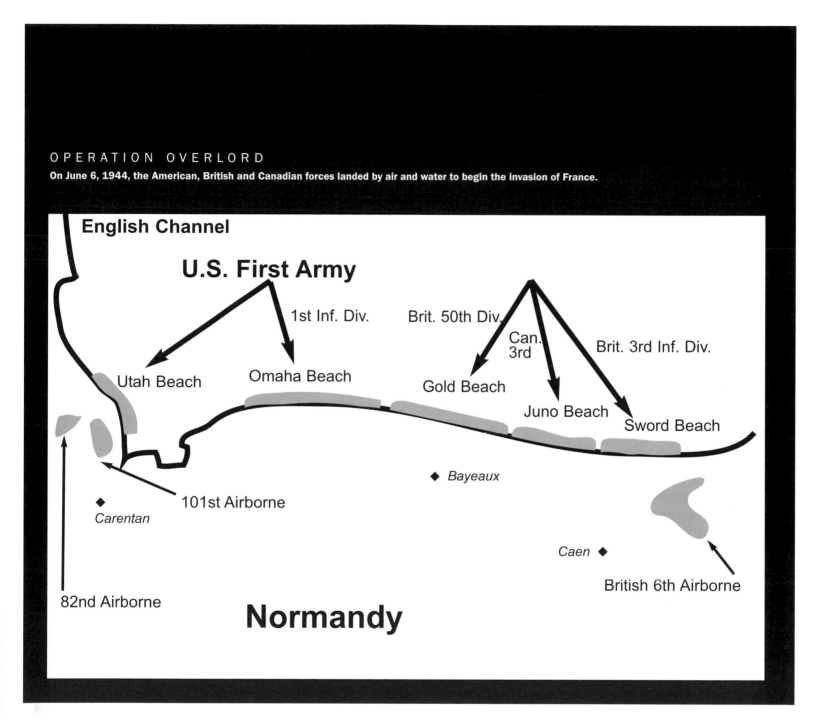

OPERATION OVERLORD
On June 6, 1944, the American, British and Canadian forces landed by air and water to begin the invasion of France.

English Channel

U.S. First Army

1st Inf. Div.

Brit. 50th Div.

Can. 3rd

Brit. 3rd Inf. Div.

Utah Beach

Omaha Beach

Gold Beach

Juno Beach

Sword Beach

◆ *Bayeaux*

101st Airborne

◆
Carentan

◆ *Caen*

British 6th Airborne

82nd Airborne

Normandy

HISTORIC GUN CREW
The sailors from Minnesota who manned the No. 3 gun on the USS Ward posed for a photo. The gun sank a Japanese submarine.

Photos from the personal collections of the crew of the USS Ward and from the book **USS Ward Fires First Shot World War II.**

FIRING THE
FIRST SHOT

The USS Ward was guarding the entrance to Pearl Harbor on the morning of December 7th 1941. The World War I vintage destroyer was manned by a crew of Naval Reservists from St. Paul. When a small submarine tried to sneak into the harbor, the Ward fired on and sank the Japanese vessel. The time was 6:45 a.m., a full hour before the Japanese air attack that precipitated the U.S. entry into World War II.

On the grounds of the Minnesota Capitol, just to the west of the Veteran's Service Building, is displayed one of the most historic artifacts in our nation's military past.

It is a 4-inch gun from the deck of the USS Ward, a destroyer that was guarding the entrance to Pearl Harbor on the morning of December 7, 1941.

The Ward, a four-stack Liberty destroyer built in the final days of World War I, appeared to be a ship of destiny from the time its keel was laid in 1918 to the time it was sunk off the Philippines in 1944.

It's place in history will always be preserved, partly because of the amazing events and coincidences that surrounded its lifetime as a ship of service in the U.S. Navy, but mainly because it fired the first shot of World War II for the United States.

Yet, that gun mounted just south of Minnesota's Vietnam Memorial is not the gun that fired that first round. That gun on the Capitol grounds fired the first round that actually hit something.

Orville Ethier was 17-years-old when a friend convinced him to join the Naval Reserve in St. Paul, and he admits that part of his motivation was the money.

"We got 70 cents a meeting, and after a while it was a dollar a meeting. In those days, that seemed like a lot of money."

Ethier joined a group of other St. Paulites at the Minnesota Boat Club near the Wabasha Street Bridge where the reserve training center was located. The men would train on small boats on the river and would spend part of their summers on larger vessels on the Great Lakes.

In late 1940, President Franklin D. Roosevelt began calling in the reserves, and the St. Paul contingent was ordered to report on January 21, 1941. Eighty-two enlisted men and two officers reported to San Diego, California, to take over the USS Ward.

The Ward was one of several hundred mothballed destroyers the Navy was putting back into commission as the threat of world war became greater. It was parked along Red Lead Row in San Diego Harbor, and it was the last of that group of destroyers to come out of mothballs.

"Because it was last, much of its equipment had been stolen when they were refitting the other destroyers. That was good for us because it meant we got a lot of new equipment," Ethier said.

The Ward was already a famous ship of sorts. When it was built in 1918 at the Mare Island Navy Yard in Vallejo, California, the ship builders were caught up in the rush to build America's wartime Navy. While other destroyers had been completed in several months, Master Shipfitter J.T. Moroney proposed to build Liberty Destroyer #139 in a month.

The keel was laid on May 15, 1918, and, working round the clock, the crews managed to get #139 ready in just 17 days, a record for a ship of war that will probably never be broken.

When Ethier and his fellow St. Paulites took over the Ward, they took the old ship on two shakedown cruises and then headed for Hawaii. "It took us 10 days to make it over, and that included seven days of sickness and three days of recovery. At least half the crew was sick, and I was one of them."

The Ward's berth in Pearl Harbor was just to the north of where the long line of warships were tied up, an area usually known as Battleship Row.

Ethier recalled that the St. Paul crew had a wide difference in their naval experience. Some were old salts who had served in the regular Navy, while others, who had just joined the reserve, had not even gone through boot camp.

The ship was assigned, along with three other destroyers, to guard the entrance of Pearl Harbor on the island of Oahu. The ships would each spend a week steaming up and back in front of the channel entrance making sure no unauthorized vessels entered the restricted area.

On December 5, 1941, the Ward had a big event with the coming of a new captain. Lt. W.W. Outerbridge, a Navy veteran of 14 years, was getting his first command.

The Ward was supposed to be off duty, but one of its fellow destroyers had a breakdown, and Outerbridge and his ship headed out to the outer harbor before he even had a chance to unpack his bags.

It was business as usual on Sunday, Dec. 7, as the Ward criss-crossed in front of the harbor channel through the night. Soon after 4 a.m., however, just as the morning watch was starting its four-hour shift, a message was received from the minesweeper Condor:

"SIGHTED SUBMARINE ON WESTERLY COURSE SPEED NINE KNOTS."

Outerbridge was called to the bridge, and he immediately sounded general quarters.

"We got a little contact on our sonar," Ethier recalled, "but we soon lost it." The ship searched for about a half hour,

< ORVILLE ETHIER

volunteered for the Naval Reserves in Minnesota when he was 17.

> ETHIER SERVED ON THE WARD

until it was sunk in 1944. He is often the spokesman for the First Shot group.

and Outerbridge ordered the crew to stand down from general quarters.

"A few hours later, they sounded general quarters again," Ethier said. "I think everyone thought it was just another drill."

But it wasn't a drill. Signalman Second Class Herbert Raeubig, the helmsman, had spotted something in the water between the USS Antares, just entering the port, and a large barge the ship was towing. The crew on the bridge at first thought it to be a drifting buoy, but then realized it was moving along at the same speed as the Antares.

Fireman Second Class Russ Reetz, a St. Paulite whose battle station was midship repair, had been in the shower when the first general quarters was sounded. This time, he was in bed. He and one other sailor took their stations amidships. "We were standing by the potato locker, and we saw what looked like a conning tower."

As the crew scrambled to their battle stations, the moving object also attracted the attention of a Navy patrol plane. The PBY Catalina circled what appeared to be a miniature conning tower, and later dropped smoke bombs to mark its position.

What the crew of the Ward did not know was that there were five Japanese miniature submarines attacking early that morning in advance of a major air strike that was to follow. The major goal of the mini-sub attack, Ethier said, was to sink a major ship -- preferably in the narrow channel leading into Pearl Harbor -- and stop the U.S. fleet from being able to put to sea.

On his way to the engine room, Ethier saw men on deck pointing at something in the water. The miniature sub was apparently following the Antares into the harbor.

Outerbridge didn't hesitate. He ordered the guns loaded with live ammunition, and he called for full speed ahead. "That was the biggest surprise," Ethier said. "We had never used live ammo."

He said he heard later that the captain had ordered the crew to, "Sink it. I may be a bum tomorrow, but it doesn't belong there." The sub was in a restricted zone where all submarines had to be on the surface. Number 1 gun, positioned at the bow of the Ward, fired first. Its shot, the first of the United States in World War II, just missed the target.

Gun 3, on the starboard side of the destroyer, fired next. The range by this time was about 50 yards, and all those months of practice paid off. The gunners made a direct hit on the conning tower. The sub began to go down.

St. Paul's Ray Nolde, a seaman first class, was assigned to Gun No. 3. "When they gave the order to fire, we were kind of dumbfounded. We thought the dang captain was crazy."

As the Ward passed by the position of the sub, four depth charges were dropped. The submarine came to the surface, rolled over, and sank. The Ward radioed headquarters:

"WE HAVE ATTACKED, FIRED UPON AND DROPPED DEPTH CHARGES UPON SUBMARINE OPERATING IN DEFENSIVE SEA AREA."

The message was sent at 6:45 a.m., a full hour before the surprise Japanese air attack that brought the U.S. into the war. To this day, Ethier doesn't understand why there was so little response by naval commanders to the message.

"Even if they had responded, it wouldn't have stopped the attack, of course. But it might have allowed the ships and the men ashore to be a little better prepared. As it was, we only shot down 29 of their planes that day."

The Ward continued to steam around the harbor after sinking the sub, picking up soundings from what may or may not have been more submarines. "We dropped every one of our depth charges -- on subs, on fish, on whatever else was down there," Ethier said.

Meanwhile, those aboard the ship could see a great deal

SMOKE POURS FROM THE WARD
after the ship was hit by a Japanese kamikaze attack in 1944. The Ward had a long career as a troop transport before it was sunk.

Photos from the Arnold Anderson personal collection

KEEP ON
TRUCKIN'

Arnold Anderson of Montevideo was a funeral director when he got his call from Uncle Sam. He worked on both the Liberty Ships and on the famed Red Ball Express, bringing supplies to the American Army. He and his drivers dealt with extreme fatigue, midnight requisitions and an encounter with Gen. George Patton over who should get a shipment of gasoline.

Arnold Anderson was a funeral director in Montevideo when he got his notice from Uncle Sam during World War II.

After Army basic training, he was assigned to Ft. Warren in Cheyenne, Wyoming, where he found himself in a group with seven other funeral directors. They all wondered what the U.S. Army had in store for them, and how the military would use their special talents.

The Army made them truck drivers.

A graduate of the University of Minnesota, Anderson soon was accepted into Officer's Candidate School and was commissioned. His first job was to be the only Army representative on a Liberty ship carrying material overseas. He was the security officer for the cargo.

On his first voyage, the Liberty ship was returning from England empty when it ran into a huge storm.

"They had put rock ballast between decks, and during the storm, we heaved over and all the ballast shifted to the port side. We were without power and dead in the water on our side."

The crew did its best to shift the fuel and other materials to the other side. "We had to shovel the ballast material uphill." The ship made it back to Boston with a 15 degree list.

"The only good thing was that all the regular food had been destroyed, and we could only eat what was in the freezers. So we had bread, milk, ice cream and steak for the rest of the trip."

That wasn't Anderson's most dangerous voyage, though. On his third trip over, he was assigned to an old World War I ship carrying 10,000 tons of ammunition. "You didn't want to use a good ship for ammunition. That crew wasn't the greatest because they basically all were Shanghaied. Nobody volunteered for that ship. The captain stayed drunk most of the time, and I didn't blame him."

In all, the ship broke down 17 times in its passage over, and spent much of its time either waiting for another convoy to come along or trying to catch up to a convoy that had left it behind.

At one point, as they were lagging behind a convoy, the crew suddenly noticed an American destroyer heading for them at full steam. "We had the black ball flying from the mast indicating we were loaded with explosives, and we were all standing there trying to wave him off."

The destroyer would not be deterred, though. It

pulled alongside the ammo ship and began dropping depth charges, hoping to destroy a German U-boat it had picked up on its sonar.

"That was a real nail-biting time."

Anderson applied for a transfer from the security business and was assigned to the 3609th Truck Company. He was in charge of 48 one-and-one-half ton Chevy trucks and 48 three-ton trailers.

Anderson joined the company in June 1944, and the next month the unit and its tractors and trailers were sent to Utah Beach in France. "We had our trailers loaded on these floating barges they called "rhinos." We missed the tide and had to wait overnight before we could land.

"The German planes started to bomb us. That's an awful feeling trying to dig a hole in a steel barge."

The company's first duties were to haul supplies from the beach to inland depots. Later the port at Cherbourg was opened, and supplies were hauled from there.

"In the early days we were supplying Patton's Third Army. As we drove down the roads the French people were so happy to see us, they would cheer as we went by. We had to watch out so the drivers didn't get too much cognac."

The Americans had pretty good control of the skies, but now and then a German plane would get through. "We were strafed, but it was just that hit-and-run sort of stuff."

As the lines stretched further, Anderson's company shifted from supplying the Third Army to the First Army. At one point as his truck convoy approached an intersection,

< ARNOLD ANDERSON
Serving as an officer in a truck company that was part of the Red Ball Express.

> RETIRED AS A BRIGADIER GENERAL
Anderson stayed in the National Guard after his wartime service and eventually retired as a general.

A DIVISON NEEDED 800 TONS DAILY

It was one thing to put an army of 60 divisions into Europe in 1944 and 1945. It was another thing to keep those soldiers fed and armed, keep the tanks rolling, and to make sure there were enough chocolate bars for everyone.

"It takes about 500 tons of supplies a day to keep a division going, about 800 tons if the division is on the move," said Don Williams, a military historian. Williams was a featured speaker at the World War II Round Table at the Ft. Snelling History Center. His program was called "48 million tons to Eisenhower — Logistics Support."

"But they didn't call it logistics during the war," Williams said. "They called it Services of Supply."

Williams served in the war in the Quartermaster Corps, and his main job was sewing grommets onto tent flies.

America had a great ability during the war to produce huge quantities of supplies for the Army, Navy, Marines and Air Corps, but a major problem was getting the material overseas. "Shipping was critical."

Once the Allies began to have better success in dealing with the German submarine threat, the creation of the Liberty Ship helped solve the problem of getting it over the ocean. At one point, shipyards could make a new Liberty ship every five days.

The numbers needed to fight a world war were astronomical. By the first of January 1944, several months before D-Day, there were 749,000 troops in the United Kingdom. By June, there were 1.5 million. In the end, over 60 divisions or about 3 million men and women saw combat in Europe. Over 700,000 vehicles were used.

To meet this need, the Allies had 94 depots set up, many of them along the French and Belgian coasts where the goods were unloaded. The port of Cherbourg could handle 12-14 Liberty ships every day. Early in the invasion of Europe, supplies were landed directly on the beach, as much as 25,000 tons a day.

To get the material from the coast to the front lines, sometimes over 400 miles away, several huge trucking systems were organized including the Red Ball route, the White Ball, the ABC line and the XYZ line.

A special problem as the war headed into its final months was getting supplies over the Rhine River where there were few bridges left. By the end of the war, the Allies had built 46 bridges across the river.

Anderson was confronted by no less a personage than Gen. George S. Patton himself.

"I was only wearing a soft hat, and no necktie. Because of the kind of work we were doing, we looked pretty ragged." Patton launched into the young officer for his lack of uniform discipline and threatened a court martial.

"I have to admit that he might have intimidated me a little bit. He asked me where I was going, and I said we were delivering the gasoline to the First Army. He looked at me and said, 'I think you're going this way,' pointing in the opposite direction.

"The Third Army got 40 semis of gas that day."

In late August, the Red Ball route was formed from the depots to the front lines, with one road for traffic going one way and another road set up for the return trip.

The convoys were in constant demand, and it was difficult keeping the trucks in good running order. Part of the prob-

lem was solved when the company acquired a unit of 20 German POWs, some of whom were excellent mechanics. "At first we guarded them well, but then we realized that they wouldn't go away even if we forced them."

Another part of the problem, getting parts, was alleviated by sending a GI to the depot with a three-quarter ton truck loaded with helmets, weapons, and other items that could be traded for engines, truck parts, tires, and so forth.

At one point, it was determined that a tractor had probably made its last trip. "We had to make a midnight requisition. We brought the old tractor in, swapped hoods with a new one, and drove that one out."

As the armies advanced, so did the supply lines. At one point the drivers were going 16-20 hours per trip and fatigue was becoming a major factor.

"When a driver could see that the truck ahead of him was weaving, he'd go up and give him a bump. And when the trucks couldn't make it up a steep grade, another truck would help push him over the hill from behind. Sometimes four or five trucks would be bumper to bumper, all pushing each other up the hill."

The drivers took a ten minute break every two hours, but often the time was used to fix a flat tire or to shift the cargo from a truck that had broken down. "The guys worked together so well, it was just fabulous."

One trick the drivers had was to wire their C-rations to the manifold of the truck for a hot meal when they stopped. "You had to remember to punch a hole in the can or it would explode."

That phase of the trucking ended on November 9, 1944, after the unit had convoyed 74 consecutive days, stopping only for servicing the trucks and unloading. "When it was all over, I sat down and just cried. I'm sure it was just fatigue."

The truck company was then assigned 48 five-ton Internationals with trailers and ended up in Belgium on the ABC route. Ships would be unloaded in Antwerp and the material was brought to Liege before going to the front. At one point, the company was unloading a ship every day doing 12-hour round trips.

The operation was under constant threat from the German V-1 and V-2 rockets that were slamming into Antwerp regularly.

"We had many close calls. I was in a Quonset hut once when a rocket hit a stand of trees nearby. All I remember is rolling on the floor with the doorknob still in my hand.

"The worst, though, was during the Battle of the Bulge when it was so foggy and you couldn't tell where the rockets were going. It was a great psychological weapon. You could hear those pulse jets coming, and you thought every one of them was going to land in your hip pocket. A couple of my men cracked."

The convoys carried every manner of military gear, but gasoline was the primary load. A convoy could take 200,000 gallons in five-gallon cans on one trip.

On one occasion, Anderson and his unit were loading up at an ammo dump when they were attacked by a German plane. On its first run, it hit the tire on Anderson's truck. "I got my carbine out of the cab, and when he came back for a second run, I got one round off."

Afterwards, he and his men went back into the ammunition depot to put out the fires that had started. "I got some of my men Soldier's Medals for that. I suppose it was a pretty foolhardy thing to do."

A LONG LINE OF TRUCKS
stretched off into infinity, bringing the materials of war to the American troops. The trips often took from 16-20 hours and fatigue was a constant factor.

In March, 1945, Patton had pushed across the Rhine on a pontoon bridge and was in great need of gasoline. Anderson's unit, though working out of Holland, was sent south with a load of fuel.

"You could see the whole Third Army stacked up in fields. They were pretty happy to see us." Anderson said he would bring the gas forward as far as possible, including going over the pontoon bridge. Just to get through the city streets was a challenge, though, and at one point the trucks were stopped by a sharp turn through a centuries-old Roman archway.

In the end, the company was able to put cement blocks on one side of the roadway — just enough to tilt the trucks so they could edge through the archway. After that, it was the pontoon bridge.

"That's very strange driving. They had a lot of smoke to cover up what they were doing. When you drove on the bridge, it was like you were in a hole all the time. The bridge would rise up before you and after you."

In the end, the unit was able to deliver the gasoline to Patton right at the front line.

After the war ended, Anderson was sent to Berlin to help

run the transportation services there, and he was present when the Potsdam Conference was held. He was the transportation officer for the conference.

"President Truman wanted to tour around Berlin and look it over, and so we arranged for a seven-passenger Cadillac for him to drive around in." The Cadillac would be part of a motorcade that would include trucks loaded with military police. A convertible, driven by Anderson, would ride in front of the President with Secret Service and more MPs.

"As I was getting our convertible into position, I could hear voices behind me. Somebody was saying, 'I'm not riding through Berlin in any G——n hearse.'" Anderson turned around to see it was the president.

Another convertible was found, and the convoy toured Truman and his top officials around the German capital.

"It was great. On a regular basis everyday, I saw the leaders of the world, political and military."

In the end, Anderson was given a personally signed photograph of the president.

Anderson, after the service, joined the National Guard and was called up during the Korean War. He later advanced to Brigadier General with five battalions under his command.

(This story originated both from the World War II History Round Table at Ft. Snelling and through a later interview with Gen. Anderson.)

READY TO GO,

trailers fully loaded with five-gallon cans of gasoline await shipment to the front. This depot was located near the beach at Normandy, with the English Channel in the background.

A LESSON IN SURVIVAL
AT THE BULGE

Charlie Haug of Sleepy Eye found himself in the peaceful Ardennes Forest in December of 1944, apparently in the backwater of the great American and British offensive toward Germany. But on Dec. 16, all that changed as thousands of Germans steamrolled over the American lines in what later was called the Battle of the Bulge. Ten days later, Haug led a small group in a desperate surrender bid.

Private First Class Charlie Haug of Sleepy Eye, Minnesota, started his World War II combat career by manning a foxhole in a company of 200 men along the peaceful Ardennes front.

Little happened for several weeks until early one morning when an eerie "moonlight" lit up the sky. It was December 16, 1944.

Ten days later, he was one of a group of eight men, three of them severely wounded, who were struggling through the snow and trees trying to find the American lines.

"No matter which way we went, we ran into Germans," Haug recalled. "The woods were full of small groups of Americans trying to survive."

Haug and the rest of the small band pressed on until it was clear the wounded could no longer travel. One man, wounded in his neck, had blood dripping down that froze in icicles on his body.

"We finally decided to head into the next town we found and surrender," he said. "I was the only one left with a rifle, and the sergeant said, 'Charlie, you go first.'"

Weak from hunger and reeling from the events of the past days, Haug stumbled toward the nearest house in a village. As he got near, he was stopped by an ominous and loud "Halt!" that came from one of the windows.

Haug threw down his rifle, put up his arms and waited to be taken prisoner. Instead a voice boomed out of the house, "Who the hell are you?"

It turned out that Haug and the others were attempting to surrender to the U.S. 82nd Airborne which had captured the town a few hours earlier with about 1,000 troops. Within hours, the men were fed, the wounded were sent to the rear, and Charlie Haug was back on the offensive in one of the largest battles of World War II.

It was the Battle of the Bulge.

PFC Charles Haug had been in the army for about a year and a half when he was sent overseas on a troop carrier. Each man had just been issued new clothes and a new rifle, and all 4,000 on the ship were being sent as replacements in units that had been shot up during the Allied advance across northern Europe to the gates of Germany.

The 28th Division, Haug's destination, had been especially hit hard during the bloody and brutal fighting in the Hurtgen Forest over a period of sev-

A TRAVELING MESS STATION

allowed the Marines to get a hot meal while out in the jungle.

Did he get a medal? "No I'm not a medal kind of guy."
"You talk about heroism. When we landed, Chesty Puller's
outfit was supposed to land on our right. Instead, they
ended up on our left because of all the confusion. There
was lead flying everywhere, and you couldn't be exposed
for a second without getting hit. But Puller went from foxhole to foxhole getting the men to move over to where they
should be. I don't know anybody that could have done
that, and he did get severely wounded. It was incredible."

Johnson's last duty of the war was actually in Japan. He
had become the intelligence officer of his unit and was
involved in the planning of the invasion of the Japanese
home islands. When the surrender was signed, he was
sent to Kyushu, the southern Japanese island, where he
went from town to town accepting the surrender of the
local militia.

After the war, he graduated from law school. He and Orville
Freeman were best men at each other's weddings.
Johnson became a municipal judge in 1948 and from
1950 to 1982 he was Anoka County Attorney. He served
as president of the National District Attorneys Association
and also of the Minnesota County Attorneys Association.
Does he plan to retire soon? Johnson shrugs his shoulders. "I just come to work everyday. I enjoy it."

HEADQUARTERS

for Johnson's divison was a series of tents in the jungle at Guadalcanal.
Note the air raid shelter in the foreground.

A MEMORIAL SERVICE

was attended by all the Marines of the 2nd Division before they left
Gaudalcanal. Over 1,000 Americans were killed on the island.

ANTI AIRCRAFT BATTERIES

were set around Henderson Field at Guadalcanal.

GUADALCANAL: THE FIRST BRUTAL STOP ON THE ROAD TO TOKYO

The first eight months of World War II in the Pacific were owned by the Japanese military forces.

The Rising Sun had, except for the Battle of Midway, seen nothing but success as its empire grew week by week. By August, 1942, that empire included Korea, vast stretches of China, Burma, Thailand, Indochina, Sumatra, Borneo, Java, and the northern half of New Guinea. Australia was being threatened.

A system of Coastwatchers, set up by Australia in prior years, reported to the Allies in May that the Japanese were building an airbase on the island of Guadalcanal in the western end of the 900-mile-long Solomons chain. Such an airbase would extend the Japanese ability to attack to the west, and would threaten the major sealanes to Australia.

Operation Watchtower was planned by the U.S. high command as a way to retake Guadalcanal and deny the airbase to the enemy. Because of the low priority of the Pacific campaign, compared to Europe, the operation became known to those involved as Operation Shoestring.

The 19,000-man First Marine Division was chosen to land on the island with the help of the 82-ship Task Force 61 of the Navy. Maj. Gen. Alexander Vandergrift led the Marine force when they landed unopposed on August 7, 1942. It was the first American ground offensive of the war.

The Japanese construction workers and handful of military personnel were surprised by the landing and abandoned the airfield and headed into the jungle.

Guadalcanal is an island about 90 miles east to west, and about 35 miles deep. The airfield was captured intact including the nearly 2,600 foot runway, over 100 trucks, and an icemaking plant the Marines quickly renamed Tojo's Ice Factory.

The Marines were ashore, but they were on their own. There was no air support or sea support, and every-day their four-mile beachhead was attacked from the air and shelled from passing Japanese ships.

Using Japanese equipment, the airfield was complet-ed in two weeks, and American planes arrived August 20.

The arrival of air support was just in time as the Japanese began the attempt to retake the airfield. A unit of 1,000 Japanese were set ashore at Taivu Point, to the east of the U.S. beachhead.

Either out of supreme overconfidence — the Japanese army had never lost a battle since the beginning of the war -- or a gross underestimation of the U.S. strength, the Japanese attacked immediately in the dead of night at a small river near Henderson Field.

The result was disastrous. By morning, 800 Japanese were dead and their commander killed himself.

Mosquitos, flies, other insects, drenching rains and insufferable heat began to take its toll. In the end, more Marines died of malaria than enemy bullets.

The Japanese came again, this time in greater force with 6,000 men. Again, they had great difficulty with the terrain and they lost their radio and big guns in an attack by Marine raiders.

On the night of September 12, the battle of Bloody Ridge began, and although the Japanese pushed the Americans back to within 1,000 yards of the airfield, the Marines dug in and held. In October, the Japanese landed a full division on Guadalcanal. The Americans by this time had also been reinforced with more Marines and the first of the Army troops who were slated to replace the Marines.

The main attack this time came from the west, but the result was the same. A furious attack was repulsed, and the Japanese were forced to retreat.

On December 9, the First Marines were taken off the island and replaced by the Second Marine Division and two Army divisions, the Americal and the 25th.

Fighting continued through January. Some of the most savage fighting in the battle took place in the hills and gullies around Mt. Austen. In the end, the Japanese evacuated 13,000 of the 36,000 troops they had sent to the island.

TYING THE FLAG TO A PIECE OF PIPE

Charles Lindberg, right, helps his fellow Marines prepare a flag for hoisting on the crest of Mt. Suribachi.

All photos by Lou Lowery, from the personal collection of Charles Lindberg.

anks for dering!

is your copy of *War Stories, Accounts of Minnesotans* ...fended Their Nation.

...-bound 184-page book is the ideal gift for a loved one, ...ool or your community library. For additional copies use ... below. Thanks for supporting the Minnesota World ...emorial.

Send me ____ copies of War Stories
$20 per book plus $2.50 each
shipping/handling
(Make checks payable to "American Legion WWII Book")

Total amount of check enclosed: $_____

Name_____

Address_____

_____

_____

Phone_____

Return to: Minnesota American Legion
              Room 300A
              20 West 12th Street
              St. Paul, MN 55155-2000

F THE

...SERS

...ry 23, 1945, that climbed to the top

...er flown over traditional Japanese soil.

...sulting photograph became the most

...eams, Lindberg is the final survivor.

...vere cheering, the ship's horns were
... I got a chill all the way through."

...g's journey to the top of the mountain
...back in Grand Forks, North Dakota, where
...r up. He had gotten a job as a teenager in
...ansporting cars from Detroit out to
...gton State, but that job quickly disap-
...at the outbreak of World War II when the
...mpanies switched over to making war vehi-

...berg joined the Marines in Seattle, went
...ugh five weeks of boot camp in San Diego,
...n volunteered for Carlson's Raiders.

...mber Col. Evans F. Carlson speaking to us
...p a truck bed. He said they were looking
...who weren't afraid to die, men who want-
...ll the enemy, and men who could march 50
... one day," Lindberg said. "So I raised my
hand."

Carlson's Raiders did additional training in
California and Hawaii, spent time at Midway Island
and at Makin Island, and eventually were home-
based at Esperito Santos in the New Hebrides.

After jungle training that lasted until October of
1942, the Raiders were landed behind enemy

well is Charles Lindberg, a retired electrician who
lives in Richfield. He was there.

In fact, Lindberg is the only survivor of the 12
Marines, six in each group, who raised the flags on
Suribachi on the fifth day of the Battle of Iwo Jima.

"You should have heard the noise from down below
when we got that flag up," Lindberg said. "The

Particularly galling was the dedication of the Marine Monument in 1954 when he and the other two survivors of the first flag raising were invited as special guests to Arlington Cemetery.

"They put the survivors of the second flag raising right down in front, and they put us way on the end, far down from dedication. Nobody paid any attention to us. They never intended to honor us. It was really a disgusting trip."

For years, Lindberg also endured the pain of actually being called a liar for claiming to have raised the first flag at Suribachi.

"I can't say if the second flag raising was posed," Lindberg said. "I wasn't there." But it was aggravating to hear the accounts of the second flag raising "stretched" in the years to come. The movie, "Sands of Iwo Jima" with John Wayne, only went further to distort the truth about the battle, he said.

"It shows all this fighting on Mt. Suribachi. The fact is, we just walked up the mountain."

The raising of the first flag started to become known and accepted in the 1960s when some military historians, using Lowery's photographs, began to tell the story. Other photographs also showed the first flag being taken down as the second flag was put up.

Since then, Lindberg said things have improved quite a bit. He now is invited to speak to schools on a regular basis in the Twin Cities, and he is invited to Marine Corps and other reunions constantly as a guest speaker.

He has been invited to Washington D.C. twice for functions, and he got to meet President Bill Clinton. In 1995, he and his wife, Vi, were invited back to Iwo Jima to attend the 50th anniversary of the battle.

This time, they drove to the top of the mountain.

"It was really great to go back there. There's a small monument on top of the mountain where we raised the flag. It's all very nice.

"They treated me like a distinguished guest."

NOT AS FAMOUS

as Joe Rosenthal's remarkable photograph of the Marines hoisting the flag atop Mt. Suribachi, this photo, nonetheless, has its own signficance. It shows the actual first planting of the flag atop the volcano – about four hours before Rosenthal's picture. The first group of Marines up the mountain never got the fame or renown as the second set of flag raisers. Lindberg is the last survivor of both groups. "Everyone who fought at Iwo Jima raised those flags," he said. Lindberg is standing at the right.

LOU LOWERY'S HISTORIC PHOTOGRAPHS

When the first flag raisers scaled Mt. Suribachi to plant the American Flag, Marine Photographer Lou Lowery of Leatherneck Magazine was there. Lowery never received the recognition or awards Joe Rosenthal of Associated Press did for his photo of the second flag raising, but Lowery's views of the Marines raising the flag and taking on the enemy atop the mountain were both dramatic and historic.

Marines crawl ashore on the infamous black sands of Iwo Jima with Mt. Suribachi towering in the background.

Four hours after the original flag was raised, a second and larger flag was put up. Lowery captured the moment of the switch.

The platoon waits for Japanese troops to exit the far side of a tunnel as Corporal Lindberg applies flames to the other side atop Suribachi.

With Lindberg in the lead, the platoon heads up the hill, stopping first to show off the flag to photographer Lowery.

Lt. Col. Chandler Johnson calls off the naval bombardment of Mt. Suribachi as the platoon gets ready to head to the summit. Johnson was later killed at Iwo Jima.

All photos are from the collection of the Family of Catherine Filippi Piccolo.

FROM KEEWATIN TO MANHATTAN

Catherine Filippi Piccolo grew up in a small northern Minnesota town, the daughter of an iron miner. Out of a group of 210 WACs at a clerk's school, she was picked for a special project. Private Filippi thought she was being sent overseas, and she was excited. Instead she was selected for a new top secret effort called the Manhattan Project. She ended up with a ringside seat to the development of the atomic bomb.

Catherine Filippi Piccolo grew up in a small town in northern Minnesota, the daughter of an iron miner.

By the time she was in her 20s, she was playing a key role in the development of the atomic bomb — first as a member of a team of WACs that handled the classified material for the Manhattan Project, and later as the officer in charge of those WACs.

"I like a challenge. I don't like to do just any job. It has to be a challenge," she said.

Piccolo grew up in a one-story house in the St. Paul Location, a tiny cluster of houses perched on the edge of an iron mine. Later the family moved a mile south to the bustling metropolis of Keewatin, a mining town with 1,300 souls.

After graduating from Keewatin High School, she attended Hibbing Junior College for a year-and-a-half before dropping out after her mother had a stroke. She took care of her four brothers and her father.

When her sister returned to Italy for health reasons in the late 1930s, Piccolo joined her for a year. In Rome, she had a chance to listen to speeches by both Adolph Hitler and Benito Mussolini.

'I was in the crowd when Hitler was talking, and I was going, 'Boo, boo, boo,' but my sister hushed me up. I said, 'I can do what I want, I'm an American citizen.' She said, 'I'm an American citizen too, but I have to live here.'"

She said there were others in the crowd who also were voicing some displeasure with Hitler, but Mussolini quieted them with a wave of his hand.

Another time at a rally for Mussolini, someone in the crowd took a shot at him, missing him by inches. "But, you know, not one word ever appeared in the newspapers about it. Not one word."

She was still in Europe when the war broke out, and she quickly headed back.

Back home in America, she volunteered for the Women's Army Corps and after basic training was sent to a clerk's school. Her dream was to be sent back to Europe.

At one point, the Army gathered 210 WACs in a room and interviewed them all. They told Piccolo, who was Private Filippi at the time, to stand off to one side. "I was so excited because I thought they were going to send me to Europe."

Instead, she was informed that she was assigned to a top secret project in New York in the Manhattan District of the Army Corp of Engineers.

When the Trinity test was successful at Alamagordo in New Mexico — the first atomic explosion — Piccolo said there was great rejoicing at Oak Ridge. "You should have seen the people dancing around."

And when the bombs were used to end the war, the crush of reporters seeking information was stunning. "We allowed 350 in for a press briefing, but there had to be another 300 at the gate who never got in because they didn't have the right credentials."

Piccolo later spent time at the Hanford Engineering Works in Washington, where they developed the plutonium for one of the two bombs. Again, she was in charge of the

FROM THEORY TO TRINITY

The theory of building a bomb that involved the splitting of atoms had been around for some time. When two German scientists in 1938 split an atom and noted how much energy was released, the theory gained significance.

The United States formed several committees, and top scientists Albert Einstein and Leo Slizard warned President Roosevelt about the practicality of making such a bomb. The "Einstein Letter" was sent, Oct. 11, 1939, and warned that such a bomb could be developed in Germany. Still, the U.S. dragged its feet for the next couple of years.

In the meantime, Germany was pressing ahead with atomic research. A heavy water plant was built, a cyclotron was nearly completed, and the Germans were massing some great scientists and engineers behind the project.

Atomic research was being conducted at universities throughout the U.S., but it wasn't until 1942 that the Manhattan Engineering District was created by the U.S. Army Corp of Engineers. It later became know as the Manhattan Project.

Still the program languished because of poor coordination and leadership. On Sept. 17, 1942, General Leslie Groves, the engineer in charge of building the Pentagon, was put in charge of the project. Groves was brash and pushy, but took immediate steps to get the project moving.

The day after he took the job, he ordered the purchase of over 1,000 tons of uranium ore from the Belgian Congo that had been stored in New York harbor. The next day, he ordered the purchase of 52,000 acres in Tennessee to build a plant to process the ore into fissionable material.

On Oct. 15, 1942, Groves named Dr. J. Robert Oppenheimer as the head of the complex at Los Alamos, New Mexico.

Enrico Fermi, an Italian who had fled his fascist homeland because his wife was Jewish, headed a team of scientists at the University of Chicago. On Dec. 2, 1942, under the west stands of the abandoned Stagg Football Field, the first controlled chain reaction was created.

Making a bomb, though, was still a theory. It was not know if uranium or plutonium would be best for the core of the bomb, and so Groves built the Oak Ridge plant in Tennessee (originally called the Clinton Engineering Works) to process uranium and the Hanford Engineering Works in Washington state to process plutonium.

The scale of the plants boggles the mind. Within months, Oak Ridge had become the fifth largest city in Tennessee with 75,000 people. The complex contained a 350-bed hospital, 55 miles of railroad, 13 supermarkets, nine drug stores and a complete school system.

Success did not come immediately, though. Several different processes were developed for creating the U-235 out of uranium ore, but none of them were working very well.

In the meantime, the Germans were also having problems with their atomic research. In June, 1942, a nuclear reactor that had been built near Liepzig exploded. The program also suffered from lack of central leadership, some scientific mistakes, and Hitler's greater interest using Germany's resources toward the rocket program.

The German program took its biggest hit, literally, in late 1944 when its heavy water operation was severely damaged by Allied bombing.

At the same time, the U.S. effort was gaining speed. By December of 1944, Oak Ridge was producing 90 grams a day of U-235. It was estimated that a bomb would need about 40 kilograms of the material.

Harry S. Truman was not informed of the Manhattan Project until President Roosevelt died, and he was not fully briefed until nearly May of 1945. On July 16th, the first atomic bomb, called "Gadget," was set off at Alamagordo testing range in New Mexico.

Two atomic bombs had been created, one using uranium and the other plutonium, and both were ready to go once enough core material was available. The bombs were dropped at Hiroshima and Nagasaki, Japan, in August 1945 and precipitated the end of the war.

In the end, the Manhattan Project had cost about $2 billion and is considered the greatest coordinated scientific project ever undertaken in the United States.

WAC detachment.

After the war, she attended an intensive schooling, along with about 50 lawyers, to learn the judge advocate's, or military lawyer's, skills.

After leaving the service, Piccolo stayed very active in the St. Paul area. She worked for several companies including two stints with 3M, interrupted because she was raising her three children. She had met her husband, who was originally from the Iron Range, in Italy. 10 years later, she married him.

She became the business manager at Hill-Murray High School for eight years, and was elected to the St. Paul School Board for two terms. She served on the St. Paul Civil Service Commission and the St. Paul Planning Commission.

She has visited Italy 14 times, and has met five different popes.

Catherine Piccolo died on Sept. 27, 2001, at the age of 85.

Editor's Note: Material for this story came from an interview with Catherine Piccolo and also from her participation in the World War II History Roundtable at the Ft. Snelling History Center.

The other short stories in this section on the Manhattan project also came from the World War II History Roundtable.

OAK RIDGE

grew from a Tennessee wilderness into a 59,000 acre complex that housed over 75,000 Army personnel during World War II. The gigantic U-shaped building was one of the production facilities for turning out fissionable U-235, used for the core of the atomic bomb. At top production, the plant could make 200 grams a day of the substance. The building was 2,450 feet long and each part of the U was 400 feet wide. The ceilings were 60 feet high.

SOME OF THE BARRACKS

and office facilities at Oak Ridge covered acres of land. At one point, over 1,000 homes were being built every month to house the workers at Oak Ridge, originally called the Clinton Engineering Works.

ON THE DEATH MARCH

Tankers from the 194th Battalion march through Bataan to prisoner camps in early 1942. Over 4,000 Americans died on the march.

All photos are from the personal collection of Ken Porwoll.

THE BATAAN
DEATH MARCH

Ken Porwoll joined the National Guard in part to look good at the annual dance. In 1941, though, the unit was federalized and Porwoll found himself a tank commander in the Philippines. When the forces at Bataan surrendered, Porwoll and 12,000 other Americans were marched for days with little food or water to prison camps where the conditions were not much better.

Ken Porwoll joined the National Guard so he could look spiffy at a New Year's Eve dance held in Brainerd.

Seven years later he had survived the Bataan Death March and four and one-half years of imprisonment by the Japanese.

Porwoll admits that his entrance into the 34th Tank Company, later part of the 194th Tank Battalion, in 1938 had little to do with higher motives.

"The National Guard sponsored a dance every New Year's, and it was the biggest social event of the winter. If you joined the Guard, you got a new uniform to wear to the dance. That was the incentive for three or four of us who signed up."

Once in the Guard, Porwoll said he enjoyed learning to operate a tank and do other military tasks.

When the unit was federalized in 1941, Porwoll was a tank commander. Three companies were sent to Ft. Lewis, Washington, for additional training.

In late September of 1941, the 194th was ordered to the Philippines. "All my life I'd dreamed of going to the South Seas, so I thought, 'Now I'm going to get a free trip.'"

The battalion, including 54 tanks, unloaded at Pier 7 in Manila Harbor and was sent to Ft. Stotsenberg about 100 miles away.

Porwoll recalls very little anticipation that war was imminent. "Our only urgency was to get our equipment clean. It was covered with that Marfax grease."

Lt. Col. Ernest Miller commanded the unit, but was unable through normal requisition channels to get ammunition for the tanks or the unit's rifles. "When the guards ended their watch, they'd pass their ammunition to the guy replacing them."

Lt. Col. Ernest Miller

Another problem was that the unit had trained in one type of tank, and was now assigned to a different model. "We weren't trained; we didn't know our equipment. It was pretty much a disaster."

On December 8th, 1941, word came at breakfast that Pearl Harbor had been bombed. The 194th's tanks deployed around Clark Field. Miller quit asking for ammunition, and simply went and got it from the ammo depot.

A REUNION OF THE 194TH TANK BATTALION

took place on the streets of Brainerd after the war. All present, except for the nurse, were prisoners of war in World War II. Porwoll is third from the right.

arrangements for Minnesotans to be released.

"We were out of there two days after the Missouri docked."

He spent time at Okinawa and the Philippines and then spent a year in U.S. hospitals getting a spinal fusion.

He is retired after 30 years working for Capitol Gears in St. Paul, and he lives in Roseville.

"People ask me all the time if I've forgiven the Japanese. I have, I really have. But I'll tell you, sometimes I have to forgive them two or three times a month because it still recycles."

Porwoll has many stories about four and one-half years of captivity, but he says there's one that he will usually share, particularly if he's talking to children.

"There was a fellow named John Faulkner who was a big guy. He had given up hope and had turned himself in to what was called the "zero ward" for prisoners at the end of

the line. He was laying there naked, because they figured you didn't need anything if you were just there to die.

"A few of us went to visit him, but we couldn't convince him to try and save himself. He just wanted to die.

"One day a fellow we didn't know came by and saw John. He said, 'I bet you're getting cold at night just laying there. Here, you can have my half a blanket.'

"The next time we came to see John, he was sitting up. He said, 'That guy just gave me the most precious thing he owned. Maybe I am worth something.'"

Faulkner began to make an effort to survive, and he did. He was repatriated and went on to have four kids and become a school teacher.

"When I speak to people about my experiences, I tell them that story and ask them to reach out to strangers. You've got to reach out. You never know when you help somebody, maybe 50 years later they will be talking about you."

IN 2002, A PLAQUE

was dedicated to the 194th Tank Battalion and others who participated in the Bataan Death March. The plaque is located at the Minnesota Capitol.

A LETTER HOME

from Porwoll to his mother had the words "hungry" and "I've lost weight" removed by the Japanese censor. The letter was written in Japan.

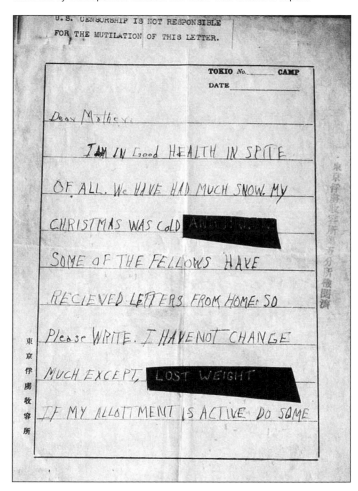

PORWOLL'S TANK

is cleverly camouflaged by a palm tree in the Philippines in 1941.

ON THEIR WAY TO THE PACIFIC

The Number Six Close Support Bomber Control unit posed for a photo while en route to Singapore in 1941. Many of the men became POWs. James Whittaker is at the top on the left in the pith Helmet.

All photos are from the personal collection of Jim Whittaker

THE BRITISH-SUMATRA BATTALION

Jim Whittaker grew up in England, and jumped at the chance to join the British Army as a signalman in 1938. In 1941, he was sent to Singapore just before the port fell to the Japanese. As a member of the British-Sumatra Battalion, a prisoner-of-war unit, he helped build the famous 'Bridge over the River Kwai.' Nearly one-third of the Battalion died by the end of the war.

No, they did not whistle on their way to work. No, the Bridge spanning the River Kwai was not engineered by a British officer.

And, no, the bridge was not destroyed by commandos, but by Allied bombers.

Despite those slight historical discrepancies, Jim Whittaker still enjoyed watching "The Bridge on the River Kwai" and has seen it several times. He is okay with the fact that the Oscar-winning motion picture bears little resemblance in some areas to the real construction of that bridge or of the Burma-Siam Railroad.

And he should know. He was there.

Brooklyn Center resident James Whittaker grew up in Manchester, England, and life was no bed of roses for him. His father, a double-decker bus driver, left the family, and when his mother got sick and was no longer able to work, Whittaker spent several years in an orphanage.

On his 14th birthday, he quit school and went to work making deliveries on a bicycle for $2 for a 60-hour week. He also worked as a wall and floor tiler and then as a roller polisher for a fabric company.

When he was old enough to join the Army in 1938 at age 17, he jumped at the chance. "The Army sounded pretty good to me."

After basic training, Whittaker joined the Royal Corps of Signals, similar to the U.S. Army Signal Corps. The transfer meant he had to sign up for a full eight-year enlistment. He did training as a radio operator, but also learned more primitive methods of getting the message across including flags, lamps, heliograph (mirror) and sounder (telegraph key).

While war for the United States still seemed far away in 1938, in England the threat of war was much more imminent. Whittaker joined the service at about the same time that British Prime Minister Chamberlain uttered his famous "peace in our time" statement.

Germany invaded Poland and France in 1939 and war broke out all across Europe. Germany began heavy bombing of English cities. Whittaker's class was hurried through radio school. "They cut out all the theory and just gave us the basics."

He was assigned to London as a radio operator, and his duty included manning a radio on the London docks during the Blitz and the Battle of Britain. "We would listen to the pilots talking on our radios. The docks were the prime target for the Germans and so there were bombs going off all around us."

Whittaker asked to be transferred overseas, and in September of 1941 he got his wish. He arrived in Singapore just 10 days before the attack on Pearl Harbor and the Japanese attacks on Allied strongholds across the Pacific. He was attached to the No. Six Close Support Bomber Control.

The unit was supposed to provide British bomber pilots with accurate information from the ground. "But nobody ever really figured out how we were supposed to do that. I don't think a pilot had time to read Morse Code at 300 miles an hour."

Singapore was a major target of the Japanese Army and Navy, and the Japanese forces moved quickly down the Malay Peninsula toward the island fortress at its tip.

Whittaker had one close brush with the invaders. His small unit was sent up the coast to help out another British unit at a small town, "But nobody had anything for us to do." They were sent out of the town and told to get a good night's sleep and come back in the morning.

When they came back, they found that the Japanese had been through the town during the night. The British office was empty and a food dump in the town was on fire. The men loaded what canned goods they could on their truck and headed back to Singapore in a hurry.

That was as close as Whittaker came to the action during the campaign. "I never fired a shot in anger. The only thing I did that remotely helped the war effort was when they ordered us to go to a Naval base on the north end of the island and remove radar equipment." It turned out later that the equipment the men brought back may have included one of the "purple machines," top-secret Japanese code breakers on loan from the Americans.

Though the British and Australians fought valiantly, it was clear that Singapore was doomed. The Allies tried to evacuate, but few ships were available. "My group of nine sat on the dock for three days waiting for a ship, but it never came." In the end, one of the members of the group managed to obtain a Royal Air Force launch. Gasoline was appropriated, and the unit headed off toward the large island of Sumatra to the south.

"We only had a vague idea of where Sumatra was, and we had no map and no compass. Somehow we went right through the mines in the harbor. It was just dumb luck."

They made their way to Sumatra, controlled by the Dutch, and crossed the island to the city of Padang where the British had made prior arrangements for rescue. Unfortunately, the last rescue boat had been there three days before. "We waited every night for another boat, but it

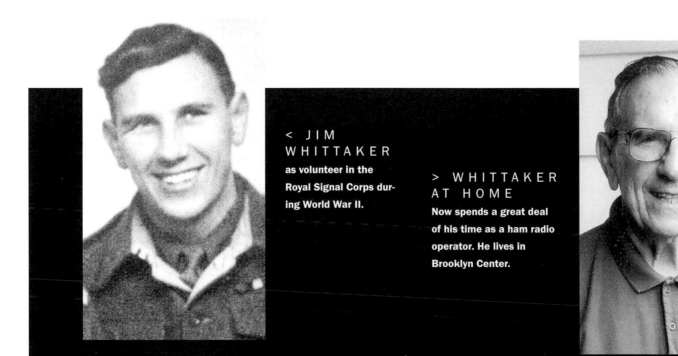

< JIM WHITTAKER
as volunteer in the Royal Signal Corps during World War II.

> WHITTAKER AT HOME
Now spends a great deal of his time as a ham radio operator. He lives in Brooklyn Center.

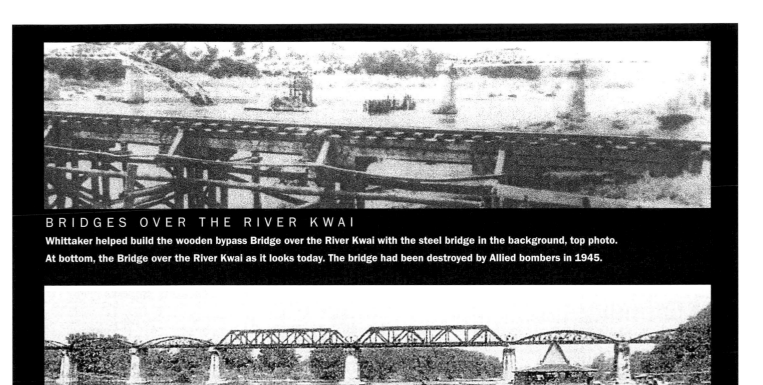

BRIDGES OVER THE RIVER KWAI

Whittaker helped build the wooden bypass Bridge over the River Kwai with the steel bridge in the background, top photo. At bottom, the Bridge over the River Kwai as it looks today. The bridge had been destroyed by Allied bombers in 1945.

didn't happen."

The Dutch were not happy to see the British troops. They had enough trouble as the Japanese were quickly taking over Sumatra as well.

As the Japanese entered Padang, Whittaker and four others went down the coast south of Padang where they were told rescue might be at hand if they made it out to an island off the coast. Natives helped them get to an island, accurately called "Mosquito Island," and left them there. They lived on turtle eggs and coconuts and battled the mosquitoes, day and night.

"All five of us came down with malaria," Whittaker said.

One day a Dutch patrol boat showed up, and the captain began talking to the British soldiers, but as he did so, troops snuck behind the Brits and captured them. "I can't blame the Dutch. They had to obey the Japs."

They were taken back to the mainland and put in a barracks with 1,100 other British and Australian prisoners of war. "At first, we thought the Japanese were funny, little guys in scruffy uniforms." That opinion quickly changed when the men were ordered to bow and salute any Japanese who came through their area. "One guy didn't,

and they beat the crap out of him."

The real problem at that point, Whittaker said, was that the Japanese had no provision for taking prisoners of war and no facilities had been prepared. "It wasn't part of their military code. They didn't believe in them."

In May, 500 men of what was called the British-Sumatra Battalion were sent to Burma, and Whittaker was among them. Conditions on the ship were appalling and many of the men were already sick with malaria. As the trip continued, dysentery was common. "The ship was pretty smelly, as you can imagine."

When they arrived, they were joined by 1,000 Australians and crowded into a small high school compound. "There were no provisions, no quarters, and there were two water faucets to serve all those men. We started to lose a lot of guys."

The railroad, from Bangkok, Siam, to Burma was deemed necessary by the Japanese in order to supply their troops there and also as part of a long-range plan to invade India. The 230 miles of rail line would have to go through some of the worst jungle in the world, and it was estimated by civilian engineers to be a four-year project. The Japanese military demanded it be done in one year.

All photos are from the personal collections of Bob Watson and Harry Burke

MAKING A STAND ON
FOX HILL

When the Chinese Army attacked the U.S. troops at the Chosin Reservoir in Korea in November 1950, the Americans had to fight their way south, battling the Chinese, the weather and the terrain. Along the way, a small band of Marines was given the job of holding a critical pass in the mountains. Harry Burke was part of Fox Company, holding the pass, and Bob Watson was part of the unit that came to the rescue.

Harry Burke thought it was pretty neat that he and a few others were ordered to sleep in a hut on that cold night in late November in Korea.

"We figured we were really getting away with something. We had a roof over our head. We were only on watch for a half hour each. The rest of the company was up on the hill grousing and griping about trying to dig in among the rocks."

As it turned out, being down next to the road that night wasn't the best place to be in Fox Company, Second Battalion, Seventh Regiment, First Marine Division.

"I even took off my clothes that night. I got in my sleeping bag, and I was sleeping good," Burke recalled. "But at about 2:30 a.m., there were Chinamen shooting all over the place. I woke up to bullets zinging over my head."

Burke dressed as well as he could under the circumstances. "I had my boots on the wrong feet, but it didn't make much difference." He headed up the hill with his bazooka, firing his .45 pistol as he went.

Before he left, he stuffed his sleeping bag and pack into a large cooking pot in the hut.

As the Marines dug in a little deeper on the hill, the Chinese soldiers called out from the hut below, "Hey, Marine, come back and get warm gear. We won't shoot you."

After the long night's siege was over, Burke and others made their way back down to the hut. The other Marines' gear was gone, but Burke's was safe in the pot. At least he could stay a little warm in the next few days as his company defended its position, later to be known as Fox Hill, on the west side of the Chosin Reservoir during the bone chilling cold of late 1950 in Korea.

Harry Burke grew up in Clarkfield, Minnesota, and graduated from Clarkfield High School. He was working a good job in 1948 when some friends encouraged him to join the Marine Reserves.

"It didn't take much encouragement. I liked that sort of thing. I wanted to do some traveling, to see some more of this country."

Burke did three summer camps, and was on his way home from camp in a Studebaker convertible on June 25, 1950, when he and his comrades learned about the outbreak of the Korean War.

Burke was a bazooka man. "I was 21 years old

and had a lot of experience with the bazooka. We figured we would be instructors."

The unit was called up on August 19, but instructing was not the duty they got. "We were fooled. We didn't think they'd send us over that fast. But on September 21, we were landing at Inchon."

Burke's unit moved through the north side of Seoul, cutting off North Korean troops. The company reached a point 30 miles north of Seoul when it was ordered back to Inchon to board transports that would take it around to the other side of the Korean Peninsula where another major landing was planned.

The troops stayed on the Navy ships longer than anticipated during what came to be known as Operation YoYo as the convoy moved up and down the coast. There wasn't enough food aboard, and at one point the Fox Company men resorted to cooking little cakes over gas stoves.

"We had found these instant cake mixes, and several guys had cooked their cakes. When I tried it, apparently there was some leaking gas because it all blew up. My little cake got blown all over the place, and I did a backwards summersault. I didn't get hurt, but I didn't get my little cake either."

The First Marine Division finally landed at Hungnam, and began its long trek north toward the Chinese border. Along the way the Marines were given warm weather gear including down-filled mummy bags and rubber coated boots.

"They also had cold weather experts who told us how to stay alive. The guys from Minnesota understood what they were talking about, but the southern guys didn't quite understand it."

Burke's ammo carrier for his bazooka got his feet wet. "They just froze up and he was gone."

Fox Company had its Thanksgiving meal at Hagaru-ri, a small city at the southern tip of the Changjin Reservoir, called the Chosin Reservoir on the Japanese maps the Americans used.

Burke was assigned to the headquarters company where he would be available with his bazooka if a likely enemy target showed up. The company moved out of Hagaru-ri and took up a position at the Toktong Pass, a critical bend in the road that must be held if the rest of the two Marine regiments advancing further north along the west side of the reservoir would have a route of escape.

The men dug in on the 27th of November, the day that Burke and the rest of the headquarters group were so happy they had been assigned a hut down by the road to sleep in.

That night the Marines fought off attack after attack by the 59th Chinese Division. In the morning, it was determined

< HARRY BURKE

opens a "Care" package from home while on duty with the Marines.

> BURKE RETIRED IN 1997

and now lives in Bloomington.

that 19 Americans were dead and over 50 wounded. But the Marines had held the high ground overlooking the pass.

Orders were given to fight their way out of the position and return to Hagaru-ri, but the company's commander, Captain William E. Barber, chose to stay and defend the position. He later was awarded the Medal of Honor.

Burke spent that first night and day helping the wounded. They were evacuated to the huts in the morning, but then had to be brought back up the hill at night. "I felt sorry for our wounded. Some of them were in bad shape. I remember one guy in particular through all these years. He didn't want to be moved. He wanted to stay down below. He knew he was going to die. We left him propped up in a sitting position."

Parachute drops brought food and ammunition every day. "We never got enough food, but we got plenty of ammunition." Burke gave up his bazooka for a rifle. "We had plenty of weapons to choose from with so many of our men down."

Every night brought another attack, and by day the Chinese sniped at the Marines from the higher hills nearby. Fox Company dug in deeper each day, "although it was hard digging in that frozen ground."

Temperatures hit minus 25 degrees and lower at night.

On the second night, Burke was assigned to a foxhole on the back side of the hill, armed with a carbine. "The Chinamen were running and moving and trying to get into position to get us. All of a sudden there was one of them about eight feet in front of me. I shot him, and then I shot another one."

When daylight came, Burke was called out of his foxhole and told to bring his bazooka to a position where they could lob a shell eight or nine hundred yards to a Chinese position. "We thought it was worth a try."

The team loaded the bazooka and Burke elevated the weapon to hoist the rocket into the enemy emplacement. A second team readied their bazooka to fire at the same time. "There was a warning written on it that said, 'Do not fire below minus 20 degrees.' I found out why."

Because of the extreme cold, the rocket was still burning as it came out of the tube. "It rolled me right over. The corpsman came over and looked at our faces. They were all seared with the hair burnt off. He just put a little vaseline on and sent us back to our positions. We fired two rounds with those bazookas, and that was it."

A VIEW FROM A FOXHOLE

was given to Burke years after the Korean War at a reunion. The photo was actually taken from Burke's foxhole on Fox Hill and shows the ridge beyond. Marines defending the pass faced constant sniper fire from the high ground around their position.

Burke said there were usually two men in a foxhole. To keep warm, the men would line the holes with parachutes from the airdrops and with blankets taken off the Chinese killed in action. "We were dug in good, and we were dug in deep. We'd share a sleeping bag as we kept watch."

On the third night, nobody came at Burke's position at first, but then he could hear shooting nearby. "The next thing I know, they're shooting right at me. I peeked out, but a bullet went by, inches from my ear. There was a log in front of my hole, and I took off my gloves and put them on top of it. A few seconds later, they were hit. One landed on my helmet, and the other landed in my lap."

A gunnery sergeant came to see what all the hollering was about. "We told him to get down, but he came right over. The next thing I know, he fell right on top of me, he'd been shot in the hand."

Another visitor the men had at various times was Captain Barber, who had been wounded twice, but still hobbled from position to position checking on his men. "The captain didn't want to give up his command. The first time he came by, he didn't want any help, but the second time he stumbled and yelled at a Marine that was with him, "Dammit, kid, can't you see I need some help?""

Burke was impressed with Barber, who had only joined the company a few weeks earlier. "He was a good leader, and

"We heard Fox Company had been riddled, and was down to a small percentage of survivors. We also knew that if they gave up their position, there would be no way for us to get back. The decision was made to send the First Battalion to relieve Fox Company."

The battalion left late in the day. It did not head down the road but instead went over the hilly terrain in a direct line to Fox Hill. "It was slow going this time. Sometimes it was one step forward and two steps back. We had to hold onto the parka of the guy in front of us, and hold onto a branch of a shrub with the other hand. There were about 500 of us on the march, and I was hanging close to Col. Davis."

The troops maintained a strict silence as they covered the miles through the darkness with Chinese troops all around. They could see the Chinese firing mortar rounds into the convoy below, but could do nothing about it because of the risk of jeopardizing their mission.

"Several times, Col. Davis would get under his poncho to take a compass reading. By the time he'd come out from under the poncho, he'd have forgotten the reading. The cold was that bitter. It was nearly impossible to concentrate."

Watson was often sent forward with messages to the company commanders. The messages usually were brief and to the point: "Slow down," "What's the hold up?" or "Take a break."

"Everyone was in a weakened condition, both from the numbing cold and also from the fact our C-rations and water were frozen solid and we had nothing to eat or drink."

The First Battalion finally made contact with Fox Company, and joined them on December 2. Men from the First Battalion immediately filled in the weak spots on the line.

"I remember the next morning seeing the huge pile of dead bodies stacked up like piles of wood." Watson also witnessed the battalion surgeon coming out of a medical tent and being felled by a single sniper's bullet.

"At one time, a helicopter flew overhead, and all of a sudden, its rotors quit spiraling. It crashed down just a few yards from where we were standing."

Watson recalled that the corpsmen would carry four surrettes of morphine in their mouth to keep the drugs from freezing.

Air drops kept the Marines supplied, mainly with ammunition. "But I do remember one drop that contained freshly baked loaves of bread and Tootsie rolls. That was a good drop."

Late in the afternoon, the unit moved out with the truck convoy that was now using the pass that Fox Company had protected. They arrived in Hagaru-ri later that night. "There were a lot of us who thought we were out of the woods at

< ENJOYING THE SUNSHINE

Bob Watson was a clerk at Camp Pendleton before being sent overseas with the First Battalion of the 7th Marines.

> IN LATER YEARS

Watson was president of the Upper Midwest Chapter of the Chosin Few, a group of veterans who fought at the Chosin Reservoir in Korea.

FOX COMPANY'S HEROIC STAND

After the Inchon Landing, the momentum in the Korean War in late 1950 was all on the side of the United Nations forces.

American Marine and Army troops were landed on the east coast of Korea and headed northwest toward the Changjin Reservoir, known to the Americans as the Chosin Reservoir because it was listed that way on the Japanese maps the Americans used.

They advanced with little resistance through the town of Koto-ri and up to Hagaru-ri, on the southern tip of the huge reservoir. Two American Army Battalions made their way up the east side of the reservoir, while the 5th and 7th Regiments of the First Marine Division advanced up the west side.

It was known that Chinese troops had reinforced the faltering North Koreans, but their numbers were not known.

By late November, the Marine position had reached Yudam-ni, about 14 miles north of Hagaru-ri over a twisting, mountainous road. One of the most critical parts of the road was over the Toktong Pass, about midway between Yudam-ni and Hagaru-ri.

Fox Company of the Second Battalion, Seventh Regiment of the First Marine Division was given the job of holding the pass. Capt. William Barber scouted a location for his 218 men, and he picked out a hillside next to the road.

During the night, the 18,000 or so American troops on both sides of the reservoir were hit by seven Chinese divisions, about 70,000 troops. The battle of the Chosin Reservoir had begun.

Fox Company was alerted by a sentry at about 4 a.m. that someone was coming down the road. At first they thought it was civilians, but as they came around the bend it became clear that it was Chinese soldiers marching four abreast. Marine machine gunners took the first action.

For the next several hours, the Americans were besieged by the Chinese troops on all sides. The enemy was able to take the crest of the hill and drive the Marines down, but they were halted from going any further. There were heavy casualties on both sides and only acts of extreme heroism up and down the line saved the Marine position.

The Marines were under attack for the next five days.

A rescue mission was organized by Lt. Col. Ray Davis, who led his First Battalion over the mountainous terrain for two days, trying to get to Fox Hill. Davis' heroic mission reached Fox Hill at 11:25 a.m. on December 2. Fox Company had held the hill and preserved a clear road for the breakout of the Marines further north.

Fox Company had 26 dead, 89 wounded and three missing. There were at least 1,000 Chinese bodies around the hill, and the Marines in some places had stacked the frozen cadavers around their positions for additional protection.

It was estimated by Capt. Barber later that 4,000 Chinese had attacked, and that as many as 2,000 had died in the attacks or from artillery and air attacks.

that point, but in reality the First Marines were engaged in a heavy fire fight around Hagaru."

Watson has one good memory of Hagaru. "We went over to this tent to get some hot food. It had been a long time since we'd had hot food. It turned out it was noodles, just plain butter noodles, but, boy, it was good."

The next morning, Watson woke up sick. "I thought I could pull myself together, but Col. Davis took one look at me and said I was to be evacuated." Watson joined 4,300 sick and wounded Marines who were flown out of Hagaru on a makeshift airstrip. He was transported to another part of

Korea, and then to a hospital in Japan. He had pneumonia.

After recuperating, Watson came back to be Davis' runner again, and when Davis was made the executive officer of the regiment, Watson stayed with him. In June of 1951, he was rotated back to the United States.

Watson served 12 years in the Marines before returning to St. Paul where he worked for the Post Office and later as an iron worker. He and his wife, Gayle, have five children.

Watson has been president of the Upper Midwest Chapter of the Chosin Few.

A BRIEF BUT MEMORABLE EXPERIENCE

Joe Ohman's tour in Korea only lasted a few weeks before he was blown off a hillside by a North Korean mortar shell.

Photos from the collection of Joe Ohman.

ANYTHING BUT A FORGOTTEN WAR

In the space of only a few weeks, Joe Ohman went from being an employee of Minneapolis Honeywell to training at a Marine base in California to fighting the enemy in the mountains of Korea. Standing on a hill with other Marines, Ohman realized that the North Koreans were 'walking' a mortar attack up the hillside. The next round would be right on top of them.

For Joe Ohman, it was an amazing few weeks.

As the summer of 1950 wound down, 20-year-old Ohman was employed as a stores manager at Minneapolis Honeywell.

A week later he was doing weapons training at the Marine base in San Diego, California.

Two weeks after that, he and his company were on a transport ship bound for an unknown destination.

Two weeks later he was fighting North Koreans in the mountains north of Seoul, Korea.

And two weeks after that, he was in a hospital in Japan recovering from a minor wound after a mortar round hit his position -- killing seven of his comrades.

Some have called the Korean War, "The Forgotten War." For Ohman, who spent a handful of days in Korea as a young man, it was a time he will never forget.

"You don't forget those things. The guys who were there will never forget."

Ohman grew up on the North side of Minneapolis, graduating from North High School in 1947. He was one of five brothers, all of whom served their nation in the military. At one time, three of them were on active duty in Korea.

As his high school days ended, the 17-year-old Ohman signed up with the Fourth Infantry Battalion of the U.S. Marine Corps Reserve.

Why? "My older brother told me I should."

For the next four summers, Ohman trained for two weeks at a time at Marine bases on the East Coast. In between, his unit gathered once a week on Tuesdays for drill meetings at the Naval Air Station at Wold Chamberlain Field in Minneapolis.

The fighting going on in Korea that summer seemed like a long ways away, he recalled. "We knew there was a chance we'd get called up, but we really didn't believe it. This was during the time when they pushed those guys off the beach (in southern Korea). We were pretty concerned, but it was all scuttlebutt."

At one of the unit's weekly drill meetings, the rumors came to an end. The message from headquarters contained only two lines:

"At the present time it is anticipated that all personnel of the Fourth Infantry Battalion will be called to active duty on 19 August 1950, to depart on 21 August 1950. You will arrange to terminate your present employment to coincide with this information." It was signed by Maj. C.C. Sheehan, the commander of the unit.

Ohman and the others got on board a special Pullman train headed for California, and a couple of days later arrived at Camp Pendleton.

"It seemed like we went 24 hours a day there," Ohman said. "We were getting all our gear together and we were firing all of our weapons."

Ohman had risen to sergeant by this time, in charge of a squad that manned rocket launchers.

As the two weeks at Pendleton drew to a close, men from the Fourth Infantry Battalion filled out gaps in the First and Second Battalions of the Seventh Marine Regiment, First Marine Division. The troops got on board two ships, the

Bayfield and the Okanagon, and headed out to sea.

"We thought we might be going to Hawaii. The scuttlebutt was flying around the ship, but, as usual, it was all wrong. We got to Hawaii and went right on by."

The ships landed some days later in Kobe, Japan, and the men were allowed a few hours of liberty. "There was just time for a few beers and then back on board."

The Marines still hadn't been told where their final destination was, but the fact that a poster of a North Korean communist uniform had been placed in each berthing compartment gave them a pretty good idea.

The ships landed at Inchon, about four days behind the first assault wave. Ohman said the fighting was still going on in the vicinity of Inchon, a port of Seoul, and the men could see the air strikes going on.

The men went ashore at Wolmido Island and traveled across a causeway into the Korean mainland.

< JOE OHMAN

as a young Marine at the time of the Korean War.

> ONE MEDAL CAME LATE

Ohman shows off his medals in a display made by his family. He didn't receive his Purple Heart until 1990, 40 years after his service in Korea.

"It was our job to punch through and go north of Seoul into the mountains. We would cut off the retreat of the North Koreans as they headed north."

Ohman's squad had uncrated its new rocket launchers on the ship. It was a bigger version of the launcher that had been used earlier in the Korean War when the rockets tended to bounce off the sides of the Russian-made T-34 tanks.

The Marines got into trucks in the pitch dark for their trip north. They were told not to fire back if they were fired upon. "I suppose they didn't want the North Koreans to know we were sending troops north."

The convoy didn't get far up the road before the troops could hear the heavy firing in the distance and the sound of artillery shells whistling overhead. Ohman's unit, Fox Company of the Second Battalion, 7th Marines, made it to the mountains in good order.

Ohman's nine-man squad was involved in some firefights, but no tanks appeared to challenge their rocket launchers. After a few days, his company was ordered to relieve another company that had been under fire on a hill.

When Ohman arrived, he espied a nice, white wool blanket that had been left behind by a Korean soldier. Ohman told his fox-hole partner, Lynn Davis, "At least we're going to be warm tonight."

Unfortunately, the blanket also served to attract the attention of the North Koreans positioned on a nearby hill. "Pretty soon there were these beautiful, blue-white tracers going right over our heads. For a while we wondered what they were doing, but then we realized they were marking our position for a mortar attack."

For the next two hours, mortars exploded all around the two. "We just pulled our necks down and stayed put. One of the mortars hit about 10 or 15 feet away, but we were dug in pretty good. There was all sorts of stuff flying over our heads. It all went back to that dumb white wool blanket."

Not long after that, on October 14, 1950, Ohman happened to be with a group of Marines that were firing down a hillside at the retreating enemy. Ohman watched the action for a while and then saw a mortar round hit at the base of the hill. A second mortar round hit a few seconds later about halfway up the hill.

"In a split second, I realized they were walking that mortar up the hill and that the third round would be right on top of us. In fact, I could hear it coming. Those big mortars sound

like ripping paper, and it gets louder as it gets nearer."

Ohman shouted to a fellow Marine near him, and the two took off running. "We had about three seconds I suppose, and we dove off the embankment."

At that instant, the mortar hit the Marine position. The terrific explosion left Ohman dazed. "My rifle had been destroyed. My pack looked like it had been hit by a shotgun blast. I had a nick on my leg, but mostly I had a hell of a concussion. I had a hard time hearing, and I was in a fog."

Up on the hill, the scene was devastating. "Seven of those guys were killed. Eight or ten were wounded. A few seconds earlier, I was standing right with them."

Ohman was led to a M.A.S.H. first aid station and was quickly evacuated to a hospital in Yakuska, Japan.

A few days later, he was sufficiently recovered to rejoin his outfit, but it never happened. "I was supposed to return to Korea, but the confusion in Yakuska was unreal. I got on a plane and I thought they were taking me back to Korea, but instead I was transferred to Hawaii."

Ohman spent time at Trippler General Hospital in Hawaii, and then was shipped back to the United States where he served out his active duty time.

"I consider myself a really fortunate person, especially

CHISHOLM NATIONAL GUARDSMEN GET READY TO GO
The men of Company C, 136th Regiment, 47th Division of the Minnesota National Guard posed in Chisholm just before they were called up.

All photos are from the personal collection of Ron Gornick.

ON A HILL IN KOREA, TWO CAME BACK

Sergeant Ron Gornick of Chisholm led a patrol into a no-man's land in the hills of Korea in late 1951 in search of a sniper. Instead of the sniper, the men found a North Korean bunker. When the shelling had stopped, the badly-wounded Gornick carried another soldier down the hill and back to the safety of the American lines. They were the only two survivors of the action that day.

On October 10, 1951, 19-year-old Ron Gornick was informed that two days later he was to report to the Battalion command post in order to be given a battlefield commission to second lieutenant.

On October 11, Sergeant Gornick led a patrol into the dark hills of Korea to find a sniper that was bothering the U.S. position. It was expected to be a routine mission into the no-man's-land between the North Korean and American lines.

Instead, the patrol encountered a fortified North Korean outpost. By the time the shelling stopped, Gornick and one other man, draped across Gornick's back, were the only ones to escape.

Gornick spent four and one-half months in hospitals in Japan. He never received his commission. He never set foot in Korea again.

———————

Ron Gornick was born Dec. 29, 1931, in Chisholm, Minnesota, and grew up there. His family bought a bottling plant when Gornick was a teenager, and he spent most of his non-school time in the family business.

He did go out for football for three straight years at Chisholm High School, but despite only missing one practice, he only got to play one game. "I guess I wasn't much of a jock, I was a lover," Gornick said with a smile.

One of the teachers at the high school encouraged the students to join the National Guard, and by fibbing about his age, Gornick was allowed to join when he was still in the 10th grade — he had just turned 16. "I was the youngest kid in the class."

Gornick said a lot of the guys joined for the uniform or for the prestige, and many joined just to get away from their parents for two weeks each summer. "A lot of guys had those strict parents, and it was great to get away from home."

Between school and Guard meetings, Gornick delivered the family's pop, Yorg's Beer and Kiewel's White Label to local establishments. The men of Company C, 136th Regiment, 47th Division trained at the Chisholm Field House on Wednesday nights.

The war in Korea began on June 25, 1950, a year after Gornick graduated from high school.

"I was trying to figure out whether or not I should go to college. I enjoyed driving the truck. But then the Korean War began, and that changed the complexion of things a little bit."

COMPANY C

trained in the Chisholm Fieldhouse in the years prior to the Korean War. The unit was federalized on Jan. 16, 1950.

shreds and they were full of blood. It was his first Purple Heart.

While there, the company commander invited Gornick to his tent for a cup of coffee and a little debriefing. "He told me I could stay there that night and head back in the morning. He had a bottle of Canadian Club, and it was kind of nice to have a drink with the company commander."

After returning to his squad, Gornick was informed on October 10 that he was to report to battalion headquarters on Friday, October 12, 1951, at 0900 to receive a battle-field promotion to second lieutenant. He had led 10 successful patrols, and the casualties in that sector had caused a need for officers. "We just didn't have many officers left. The fighting had been pretty intense in that area, and the officer corps had been pretty well annihilated."

Back on duty, Gornick and the rest faced what seemed like a humorous situation at first. "When people would go to the latrine, and while they were bending over the hole, a sniper was taking pot shots at them. Well, then one day a guy got snapped right square in the buttocks."

The commander told Gornick to take his squad out that night and try to locate the sniper. Squads varied in size,

but Gornick remembers that this one had a lead scout, a radio man, a medic and a stretcher bearer with it, and there were probably 15 or 17 men who headed off in the dark at five in the morning.

The men followed the scout down paths and up paths in pitch blackness, heading for the hill where it was thought the sniper was shooting from. The squad reached the top of the hill just as light was breaking. The scout signaled to move ahead slowly.

Without knowing it, the small group of soldiers moved right up to a North Korean forward artillery observation post. The enemy soldiers were located in a low, concrete bunker with horizontal slits that looked out over the American position.

"We came across them sleeping. All of a sudden, we could see heads popping up inside the bunker. We were only a few feet from them. I don't know who shot first, but then all hell broke loose."

Gornick said it was almost too close to aim and shoot rifles. The two sides were throwing grenades at each other. "They were throwing their concussion grenades, but we were too close for them to be activated. I picked up two or three of them and threw them back."

In a few minutes of furious, point-blank fighting, the squad was able to silence the bunker, but not before the North Koreans were able to call in an artillery barrage on their own position. Mortar and artillery shells came raining down on the American squad.

"Everybody was down, and everybody needed help," Gornick recalled. "One mortar came in and it got me, and it got the medic right next to me. I looked at Doc, and he said, 'Can you help me?'

"I'd been hit in the arms, in the back, in the legs. I was all torn apart. I told him I couldn't help him. Somehow I picked up his helmet and put it on his head."

In time, the barrage lifted. "It had only been 10 or 15 minutes, but it seemed like six months."

Gornick looked around. He saw one other soldier still moving. "It was a little Jewish kid from New York. His name was Oscar Viskowicz. He had a big hole in his middle. It didn't look like he was going to make it. I don't know how in the world I did it, but I grabbed the guy and threw him over my shoulder and headed down the hill. I kept falling and getting up again. I really felt sorry for that poor guy I was carrying.

"I don't remember much until I got down the hill and was

grabbed by a couple of our guys. I was losing it by that time. I didn't have enough blood left in me to stay conscious."

The next thing Gornick remembers was being strapped into the basket of a helicopter. "They took me to a Norwegian MASH unit and I was treated there. There were all kinds of people wounded that day, and the place was crowded."

He faded in and out of consciousness. At one point he awoke to find a doctor standing over him. "The doctor said, 'I have some bad news for you. We're going to have to amputate your legs.' I remember thinking, 'Holy cripes, how had I carried that guy down the hill? My bones had to be okay.'"

An ambulance took him to the airfield, and he was flown to an army hospital in Japan where he spent three months recovering. His thighs were laid open so deeply that they couldn't put in stitches, and the wounds had to close by themselves, slowly. But there was no more talk about amputation. He was moved to another hospital in Japan for rehabilitation.

"While there, a lieutenant from our company came through. He'd been plunked in the foot. All this time, I'd never known what had happened to my squad, if anybody had made it out. He told me that my squad had been all wiped out."

The thought of going back to the front line was not a happy one for Gornick. "I'll be the first to admit that the second time around I was not so eager to volunteer. But I was prepared to go back."

Gornick's discharge date was just a month off, but there had been talk that all the GIs would be extended one year.

Finally, he was able to talk to an officer at the hospital who told him his wounds were too severe for him to ever be sent back to the battlefield. A few weeks later, he was on a troop ship to California, and not long after that he was flown to Camp McCoy. It was March, 1952.

"I got home on a Saturday night. We all went up to the Tibroc Bar, and we had a celebration."

Back home, Gornick went back to work on the beer truck. Over the years he was commander of the Chisholm American Legion and VFW posts and a member of the Disabled American Veterans.

He tried through the years to find out the whereabouts of Viskowicz, the soldier he had carried down the hill. "I don't

GETTING READY TO BOARD A BUS

Gornick stopped to pose for a photo during a training session for Company C in Chisholm.

CLEANING UP

at Camp Rucker in Alabama during a field maneuver, Gornick was 19 years old when this photo was taken.

think he made it. I can still see that hole in his stomach."

Gornick received his second Purple Heart, but through an odd Army paperwork snafu, he never received his Combat Infantryman's Badge. During the few hours that he thought he was going to be a typist at the replacement depot, his MOS had been changed to clerk on his papers. No amount of convincing will change the Army's conviction that Gornick was a clerk and not an infantryman in Korea, and he has never received the award.

In time he owned his own convenience store businesses in Chisholm and Hibbing, and he has owned several other

businesses. One day he made the acquaintance of then State Senator Rudy Perpich. Gornick worked hard for Rudy's campaigns, and the two became close friends. Perpich later appointed Gornick to the Metropolitan Stadium Commission.

From 1983 to 1991, Gornick served as chairman of the commission and was involved in the process that brought the Super Bowl and the Final Four to the Metrodome.

Gornick and his wife, Carole, are now retired in Chisholm. They have two sons, Michael and Joel, and four grandchildren.

< SPORTS MEMORABILIA
has a prominent place in the Gornick home in Chisholm. He served as chairman of the Metropolitan Sports Facilities Commission during the 1990s. He is now the president of the Chisholm Community Foundation.

Chuck Ferguson shows off the proper technique for using a bayonette while one of his fellow trainees captures the moment with a camera.

Photos are from the personal collections of Chuck Ferguson and Howard Schuette.

SURVIVAL
ON TWO HILLS

Chuck Ferguson and Howard Schuette fought in different places and at different times during the Korean War, but both faced long odds in coming back alive. Ferguson was thought to be dead on Hill 334 along the Main Line of Resistance in 1951. Schuette fought at the infamous Chosin Reservoir in 1950, and still bears a scar on his right leg from a rifle bullet that struck him on Hill 1221.

Chuck Ferguson had already been wounded three times before he got tangled up in the concertina wire.

It was in the early morning hours of Thanksgiving Day, 1951, when Ferguson and a fellow GI decided their best hope of survival was to head for the bottom of the Korean hill they were defending and work their way around back to their lines.

The Red Chinese had been attacking en masse throughout the night and had nearly wiped out the platoon of soldiers guarding the exposed outpost hill.

Ferguson could only crawl by that point, with one kneecap nearly blown off, shrapnel wounds up the insides of both legs, the left side of his face a mass of exposed flesh, and a bullet wound under his arm.

His comrade made it to the bottom of the hill, but Ferguson got hopelessly tangled in the maze of barbed wire. "I must have made a noise, because a Chinese soldier came over to check it out. By this time I was laying on my back. He pointed the rifle at me, and I put my arms up and yelled, 'I surrender.'"

The enemy soldier took dead aim at Ferguson's head from two feet away and pulled the trigger.

When Chuck Ferguson arrived in Korea in 1951, the vast movements of the war were over, and static battle lines were forming.

In 1950, the North Koreans had pushed the South Koreans nearly into the sea before American reinforcements arrived. The Americans counterattacked and drove north to the Yalu River at the Chinese border before the Chinese Army intervened. The United Nation forces were forced back again before rallying in early 1951.

Ferguson arrived as a heavy weapons specialist when he landed at Inchon on September 16, 1951. He was assigned, however, as a rifleman to the First Cavalry Division and sent to a location near the Imjin River north of Seoul.

Ferguson had joined the National Guard as a high school senior in Cogswell, North Dakota, in 1949. The following year, after graduation, he took an eight-week college course and was licensed to teach at a country school in Brampton, North Dakota.

He was teaching his group of 12 students in late December 1950 when he was called up. He found out about the presidential order from a fellow Guardsman on a street in Cogswell.

"He said, 'Let's go to Barney McGraw's Bar and get a beer.' I said, 'How can we do that, we're only 18?' He said, 'We just got activated by President Truman. We're old enough now.'"

Sure enough, the bar owner, after hearing their story, honored their request.

After training at Camp Rucker in Alabama, Ferguson was among a small group that volunteered for a transfer. They were thinking of Europe, but the Far East was selected as their destination.

The young soldiers weren't that dismayed, though. "It was kind of a lark. We were only 18 years old. We didn't understand all this war business."

When he arrived with the Eighth Cavalry Regiment, Company F, Third Platoon, his unit was in an R&R status a short distance behind the front line, known in Korea as the Main Line of Resistance, or the MLR. Soon, they were back in action, and they were ordered to take Hill 334, a posi tion that stood between the Chinese and American lines.

"They told us to fix bayonets. We were yelling and hollering. To me it was just a big game. Oh, boy, this was fun." As

they were running for the hill, though, Ferguson stumbled and was nearly impaled by the soldier behind him.

"That's when it dawned on me that this was not just a game. It was deadly serious."

The Third Platoon reached its objective and took the hill, but at great cost. "We were in a trench, and the Chinese were throwing hand grenades at us. There were hordes of them, lots of them, and they kept throwing these things at us. We couldn't shoot fast enough to stop them."

At one point, Ferguson was hit in the right arm by a sniper firing from behind the American position. Despite his wound, he helped another seriously wounded soldier down the hill toward American lines.

He left the soldier in a ravine and went for help. The officer in charge ordered Ferguson back to the field hospital, and eventually the other soldier was also rescued.

Ferguson recuperated at a British MASH unit behind the lines for 30 days.

He rejoined his platoon, and not long after that had anoth- er exposure to the deadly vagaries of war. "We were head- ing for chow, and we decided to have a race down the hill to the chow line. A couple of guys didn't race, but stopped to fill their canteens at a Lister bag about halfway down. They were hit by a mortar and both killed. If we hadn't been running, we would have got it too."

< CHUCK FERGUSON joined the North Dakota National Guard as a high school senior and was called up in 1951.

> NOW RETIRED, Ferguson was employed as the state Adjutant of the Minnesota American Legion for many years.

A few weeks later, Ferguson and his mates were looking forward to Thanksgiving. On the day before Thanksgiving, November 21, 1951, they were ordered on a normal rotation to man Hill 334. The hill was an important outpost because it allowed whoever held it to monitor the enemy's lines.

The U.S. troops had spent several weeks reinforcing the position, and the hill was protected by a series of trenches -- one that went all the way around the base of the hill, and three others, like spokes on a wheel, that connected that trench to the command post at the top of the hill.

Extra rations had been shipped in, and the men were happy because they were only slated to stay on the hill for one day rather than the normal two-day stint. There was also talk of the unit being taken out of the lines and rotated home.

Ferguson was assigned to a foxhole overlooking one of the hill's spurs or fingers. He and his fellow riflemen spent part of the day reinforcing their position with sandbags, but finally had to give up the task because of sporadic enemy shelling.

As the evening wore on, the GIs hunkered down in their positions. "It was really quiet. They had given out extra rations, and so I had two. It was very peaceful."

At five minutes after 10 that night, though, all hell broke loose in the form of an artillery barrage. Over 1,000 shells hit the hill. "They hit us with everything they had, and then they attacked."

Masses of Chinese troops attacked the hill, and the Americans fought them off with machine guns, rifle fire and artillery support of their own. The enemy bodies were three and four deep in places, but the attack just kept coming.

Early on, Ferguson was hit with a bullet under his left arm. "I was wearing a bullet proof vest, and it might have glanced off that and hit me. The vest might have saved my life."

Ferguson lost all feeling in his arm. Because it was difficult for him to fire his rifle, he was assigned the job of guarding the trench for the other men manning the foxhole. They had heard that the Chinese had captured the trench at the far side of the hill, and had also taken the command post at the top of the hill.

The attack soon came from above as well as below. An enemy soldier began lobbing concussion grenades into the trench where Ferguson was sitting. "The first grenade

A VISIT FROM MOM

made the front page of the Minneapolis Tribune at Christmas time in 1951. Ferguson was in Letterman General Hospital in San Francisco, and the visit was paid for by the Army, a San Francisco newspaper and the Red Cross.

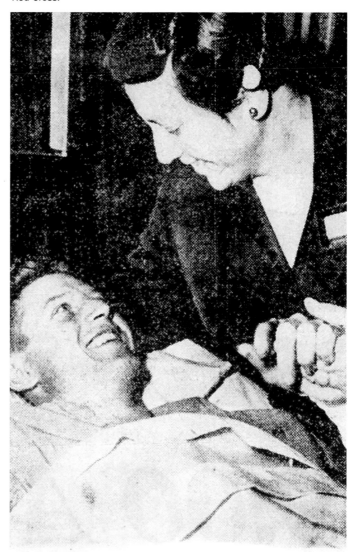

A COGSWELL, N. D., MOTHER, Mrs. ... ...m r her son, Pfc. Charles W. Ferguson at Lett nital after arriving at San Francisco by air

came in and I kicked it out with my feet while I was on my back. This happened three more times, and each time I was able to kick it out. The next time, though, it exploded right at my feet.

The blast sent shrapnel into both of Ferguson's legs, nearly removing his right knee cap. Other shrapnel hit him on the left side of the face, and blood gushed from the head wounds. "I just lay there trying to stop the bleeding on my head, and wondering why my knee hurt so bad. After a while, I just passed out."

Two hours later, he woke up and the battle was still raging. Many of the 48 men in the platoon were dead or badly wounded. Ferguson told a fellow GI that he had noticed a small cave nearby where they could take shelter, and the two men headed for it. On the way, several other grenades exploded near Ferguson, sending more shrapnel into his head. One of the grenades shattered an eardrum.

When they got to the cave, though, they found it already crowded with soldiers. "We didn't have too many options left, and so we decided to head down the hill and try and get through the wire, go all the way around the hill, and try and make it to the MLR. I was crawling on my hands and knees."

Caught in the wire, with the Chinese soldier standing above him, Ferguson figured he had breathed his last. "I kept yelling, 'I surrender,' but I don't think he understood me, and I don't think they were taking too many prisoners anyway. I saw he was using an American rifle, and it looked kind of beat up."

Despite firing from point blank range, the enemy soldier somehow missed Ferguson entirely. Ferguson put his hands up again and yelled his intentions to surrender more loudly, but the Chinese soldier fired again, this time hitting Ferguson in the right hand.

"I finally figured out that yelling wasn't working, so I just rolled over, moaned and pretended I was dead. I was amazed, but the soldier walked away and left me alone."

Ferguson again passed out. He woke up later and tried to make it back up the hill. He managed to crawl some distance, but again became unconscious.

"The next thing I remember is somebody standing over me saying, 'Hey, sarge, this one's still alive.'" The battle was over, and the medics were separating the dead from the wounded.

Ferguson was helicoptered to a hospital where he awoke for a few minutes to find a nurse cleaning him up. He apologized to the nurse for being such a mess, and slipped back into dreamland.

"I don't remember them stitching me up. I suppose I was out for two or three days." It turned out Ferguson had lost eight pints of blood on Hill 334.

Ferguson spent the next few months at Letterman General Hospital in San Francisco as his wounds healed. Just before Christmas, he got an unexpected visitor and some front page notoriety. His mom came to visit him at the hos-

pital, part of a program funded by the Army, a San Francisco newspaper and the Red Cross.

The Fergusons were on the front page of the Minneapolis Tribune on December 23, 1951. It was almost exactly one year since Chuck Ferguson had been called to active duty.

Ferguson spent nearly six months recuperating, and then was given a medical discharge. He had earned two purple hearts, two bronze stars with a V device and a unit citation during his time in service.

He returned to college, earning a teaching degree and ended his teaching career after teaching for 17 years at Crosby, Minnesota. He had been active in the American Legion for many years, and took a job as director of the American Legion's National Education program in Indianapolis in 1977.

In 1978, he returned to Minnesota to become Department Adjutant, a position he held until his retirement in 1994.

He and his late wife, Dorothy, had four children. "Right now, I do as little as possible. I like to work around the home."

Ferguson, 67, has made contact through the years with some of the men in his platoon. The 48-man unit on that day earned three Distinguished Service Crosses, 12 Silver Stars and a Medal of Honor. It was the smallest unit up to that time to earn a Presidential Unit Citation.

CLOWNING AROUND

helped pass the time at Camp Rucker for Ferguson and a friend. Not long afterwards, Ferguson volunteered for a transfer and was sent to Korea.

ONE OF THE CHOSIN FEW
HOWARD SCHUETTE USED HIS RIFLE AS A CRUTCH TO ESCAPE THE CHINESE

Howard Schuette bears a scar on his right leg, where a bullet ripped into his ankle on December 1, 1950, on Hill 1221 near the Chosin Reservoir in Korea.

He also bears a few other scars that are a little harder to see.

"I think about the Korean War all the time, although I don't know why," Schuette said at his home in Plato, Minnesota. "Sometimes I think about what the big brass did and why. I suppose they had their reasons, and I suppose that's what happens when you're sitting at a desk and you're not on the front lines.

"To me, the whole idea of the Korean War was a waste of time. And the same thing in Vietnam. If you can't finish them, don't start them.

"Although I suppose I'd do it all over again."

Schuette's most vivid memories of Korea revolve around a few days near the Chosin Reservoir in North Korea. Like many other Chosin survivors, he wonders about the American military strategy that went into the military disaster around the large, frozen reservoir.

"They just didn't know how many Chinese there were, I suppose. There were just thousands and thousands of them. We didn't stand a chance."

Schuette was a regular Army soldier whose unit had landed at Inchon earlier in the year and fought through Seoul.

He had enlisted in the army in 1949 after graduating from Glencoe High School. "I was looking for action, just wanting to get away from home." He trained at Fort Riley, Kansas, and was in preparation for Officer Candidate School when the needs in Korea took precedence.

His unit was first sent to Japan, and after a month training at the base of Mt. Fuji, the troops left for Korea.

As they headed north into Seoul, they got their first taste of action. "We were trying to clear out an old monastery, and the bullets were flying around. They were snipering at us."

At one point, Schuette encountered a North Korean soldier. "You just start shooting, it's actually pretty easy. It's you or him."

As the enemy troops fell back north of Seoul, the Seventh Division was loaded on a train and taken south to Pusan at the tip of Korea. There they were loaded on ships and taken up the coast to Iwon where they landed unopposed on October 29.

The men marched the 64 miles to the city of Hagaru, on the southern tip of the Chosin Reservoir, without encountering the enemy. The reservoir was built by the Japanese to supply Korea with electrical power.

Schuette's Able Company, part of Task Force Faith, worked its way up the east side of the reservoir and was dug in north of one of the bays of the reservoir. At first it was quiet, but on December 1 at about four in the morning, the attack began.

"The Chinese knew more than we did, and they really set us up. We didn't know much about them, but they knew all about us. I could hear the bugles, and the troops were yelling, 'Rotation Able Company. Rotation Able Company.' They knew exactly who we were."

Schuette carried a 47-lb. recoilless rifle with him, and served in the company's heavy weapons platoon. The platoon was held further back than the other platoons, and he was spared some of the overwhelming force of the attack.

At one point, Schuette had his weapon lined up on a Chinese tank only 300 yards up the road, but his commanding officer refused to give him permission to shoot it because he might expose their position. "I lugged that thing all over Korea, and that was the only time I had a chance to shoot it, and he wouldn't let me. I had that tank right where I wanted it."

What was left of Able Company retreated back to a perimeter near an extended bay of the reservoir. With their backs to the water, the GIs made a stand. "By this time, most of the first, second and third platoons were completely wiped out. The CO was dead, the command post had been hit by

HOME ON FURLOUGH
Galen Bungum had his photo taken at his family farm in Hayfield with his father and two brothers.

All photos are from the personal collection of Galen Bungum.

HE WAS A SOLDIER ONCE...
AND YOUNG

Galen Bungum grew up on a dairy farm in Hayfield, Minnesota. In 1965, he was a member of the 'Lost Platoon' during the Battle of the Ia Drang Valley, one of the key battles of the Vietnam war. The battle is the subject of the 2002 film, 'We Were Soldiers.' Cut off from their comrades, the platoon had a casualty rate of 76 percent over a two-day period.

Galen Bungum never had a notion as he trudged through the jungles of Vietnam that a Hollywood actor would someday play his part in a major movie.

Bungum grew up on a dairy farm near Hayfield, Minnesota. He milked cows seven days a week.

At Hayfield High School, he played on the football team and was in the band. He graduated in 1961, and, by 1964, the Vietnam War was heating up and the draft was going full blast. At that time, Bungum was still working at his father's farm, and also driving a milk can route every day of the week.

"A bunch of guys I went to school with were scheduled to leave in April. I checked and found out I was going to be drafted in May, so I just volunteered."

He was sent to Ft. Leonard Wood in Missouri where he found that his upbringing on the farm handling milk cans had some advantages. "They made you do the monkey bars before you got chow. I had no problem, but some of those guys just couldn't make it. Their hands were all torn up. My hands didn't do that."

After training in Missouri and at Ft. Ord in California, Bungum was sent to Ft. Benning, Georgia, where he spent the next 11-1/2 months.

He was part of the 29th Infantry Division whose major role was to provide the opposition for the Ranger School based at the camp. "They were the aggressors and we were their enemy. If they went out for 21 days, we went out for 21 days."

In July of 1965, Bungum took 21 days leave back in Minnesota. He returned to a surprise.

"I walked into the barracks and somebody told me that we were all in the First Cavalry Division. There was a bulletin board on the wall, and if your name was on it, you were going to Vietnam."

Bungum's name was on the list.

He was assigned to the First Battalion of the Seventh Cavalry — known through history as Gen. George Custer's regiment at the Battle of the Big Horn.

The division was moved to Charleston, South Carolina, where it boarded the USS Rose, a World War II vintage troop transport that made its way down the East Coast, went through the Panama Canal, and then came up the West Coast before heading for Vietnam. The 29-day cruise included a major three-day storm.

Duncan gave Bungum his canteen, and the group headed off. "I remember stumbling over a dead VC and, falling down, ending up face to face with another dead one with his eyes wide open."

The men were taken back to the command post where Col. Moore had set up his headquarters next to a large ant hill. Joe Galloway, a UPI reporter who later collaborated with Moore on a book about the Battle of the Ia Drang Valley, had also arrived by that time. "He got all of our names and talked to us as we went by."

Bungum and two others were loaded into a chopper and taken back to the base at Pleiku where they had their first meal in two days. After that, Bungum was put on another chopper that brought him back to the home base at An Khe.

"Clark wasn't with me, but I figured he was on another chopper. During the night we had been talking about cele-

brating a birthday he had coming up," Bungum recalled.

Meanwhile, Savage, Clark and two other unhurt survivors of the Lost Platoon stayed at Landing Zone X-Ray, and then were evacuated to Camp Holloway. Two nights later, they were ordered to do perimeter duty at Catecka Tea Plantation, a regimental headquarters.

That night an American howitzer round fell short of its mark and killed Clark, who was sleeping on the perimeter. He had survived the Battle of the Ia Drang Valley only to be killed by friendly fire. It was his 20th birthday.

In the end, the 2nd Platoon lost nine men killed in action and had 13 wounded for a casualty rate of 76 percent. Only seven made it through unscathed. When the battle was over, about 75 North Vietnamese bodies were counted just outside the platoon's perimeter.

Bungum recalls that Gen. Westmoreland came to talk to

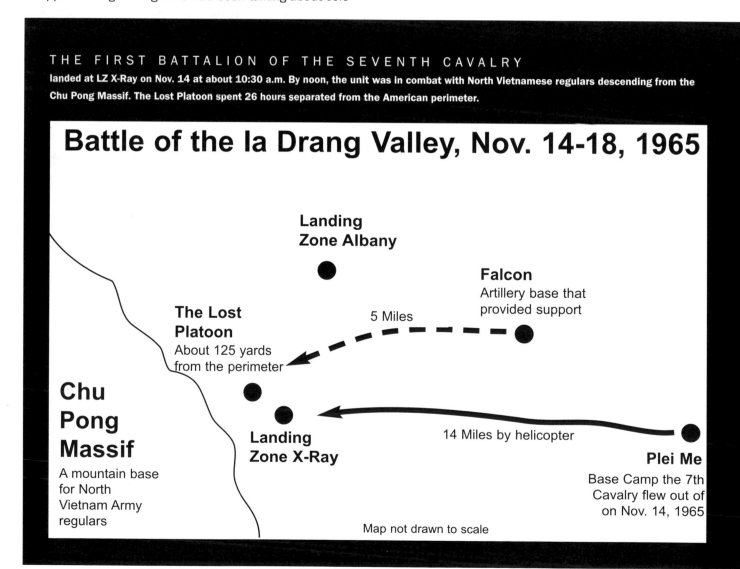

THE FIRST BATTALION OF THE SEVENTH CAVALRY
landed at LZ X-Ray on Nov. 14 at about 10:30 a.m. By noon, the unit was in combat with North Vietnamese regulars descending from the Chu Pong Massif. The Lost Platoon spent 26 hours separated from the American perimeter.

Battle of the Ia Drang Valley, Nov. 14-18, 1965

Landing Zone Albany

Falcon
Artillery base that provided support

The Lost Platoon
About 125 yards from the perimeter

5 Miles

Chu Pong Massif
A mountain base for North Vietnam Army regulars

Landing Zone X-Ray

14 Miles by helicopter

Plei Me
Base Camp the 7th Cavalry flew out of on Nov. 14, 1965

Map not drawn to scale

his battalion. The empty boots of those who had been killed were lined up. "That really got to me. I didn't hear hardly anything Gen. Westmoreland said, except we did a good job. This whole thing was hard to deal with for a long time. I couldn't sleep, and when I did I would wake up and holler. There was sweat pouring off my face."

The Battalion stayed out of action for a few weeks until replacements could be brought in for the losses. In all, the 1st Battalion of the Seventh Cavalry lost 79 killed and 121 wounded in the battle.

There were many more missions to be fought, but none with the intensity of the Ia Drang Valley. "We were up by Bong Son and what they called Happy Valley. We'd take an area and lose some guys and then pull out. And then a couple of weeks later we'd do it all again. I never understood that."

After nine months in Vietnam, Bungum's two-year enlistment in the Army ended, and he was sent to Saigon to be flown home. "While we were waiting for our flight, they took our weapons away from us. We didn't like that too much. We figured as long as we were in Vietnam, we wanted our weapons. And, sure enough, that night they shelled the airport. When our plane left the next morning, it had to swerve on the runway to avoid the bomb holes."

Bungum returned home to Hayfield in April of 1966. "At home, the effects were present for quite some time. Mom said one of my first nights home, I woke up hollering and completely tore the bed apart, ripped the new sheets to shreds."

As time went by, Bungum readapted to civilian life. He married Marcia in 1968. They have three sons, Jason, Shad and Ryan. After many years of farming, Bungum, 58, now drives a semi-truck throughout the Midwest.

The book, *We Were Soldiers Once... And Young*, came out in 1992 and described the battle of the Ia Drang Valley through the eyes of those who were there. The movie *We Were Soldiers*, based on the book, came out in 2002.

Actor Blake Heron plays the part of Spec. 4 Galen Bungum. Bungum received no compensation for the book or the movie, and is not happy that anybody would think he did.

"To this day, I can't figure out why some of us made it out of there and some didn't," Bungum said. "We all prayed as hard, fought as hard, and we were all for each other. I think about that a lot. I feel really fortunate to have survived. So many guys didn't."

IA DRANG SAW NEW TACTICS, TECHNOLOGY

The First Cavalry Division arrived in Vietnam in September of 1965 and was a pioneer of a new battle strategy concocted for the war in Vietnam. Instead of marching troops to battle, the cavalry units could be flown in by helicopter directly to the scene of the battle, avoiding ambush and attack along the way.

The 1st Battalion of the Seventh Cavalry arrived before noon on November 14, 1965, at Landing Zone X-Ray near the Chu Pong Massif, a mountainous area where North Vietnamese Army troops were based. By noon the battalion was under heavy attack, and the 2nd Platoon of Bravo Company was cut off from the U.S. perimeter.

Heavy fighting continued through the next day. The battle was also an opportunity for the U.S. forces to bring in massive firepower by artillery, jet, helicopter and even B-52 bombers.

The U.S. had nearly 200 casualties in 24 hours, but it was estimated the Vietnamese suffered over 2,000 killed or wounded.

On November 17, the Second Battalion of the 7th Cavalry, which had been called into the fight two days earlier, was marched two miles to LZ Albany for evacuation. The unit of 400 men was ambushed by NVA forces as it reached LZ Albany and suffered 155 dead and 124 wounded by the next morning. The Vietnamese avoided the U.S. air superiority by attacking at close range.

The battle was a precursor for the tactics used by both sides as the war dragged on for another 10 years.

TO MAKE A
DIFFERENCE

After striking a land mine in Vietnam, the armored personnel carrier Jon Hovde was driving was blown to pieces. Hovde woke up six days later in a hospital and his only request was that he be allowed to die. A chaplain, however, convinced Hovde to fight for his life. A terrible fever raged through his body, though, and as life ebbed away, Hovde made three vows in a pact with God.

One of the medics on the scene on January 8, 1968, found that Jon Hovde had no pulse in his left arm and pronounced him dead. The medic didn't know that the arm, still in the shirt, had been completely severed from the body.

Hovde, a member of the 25th Infantry Division, Fourth Battalion, 23rd Infantry, Company A, had been the driver of an armored personnel carrier that day in Vietnam when his vehicle struck a land mine near Cu Chi.

The mine struck the APC with such impact that the vehicle's engine was blown a half a football field's length away.

The explosion severed both Hovde's left arm and leg. His right arm and leg were so badly damaged that he received 185 wire stitches in his arm and 190 wire stitches in his leg. He also had a fractured skull and a crushed right foot.

"I don't remember anything for six days. That's when I woke up."

The waking up was not pleasant. "What I wanted to do was die. I was in intense pain. Half my body was gone. But then the chaplain walked in."

The chaplain convinced Hovde to fight for his life. He told him how many letters he had received, and

he read two of them — one from his mother and one from his girlfriend.

The letters gave him reason to live, but he was far from over the hump from his horrendous injuries.

His temperature rose to 107 degrees, and doctors ordered an ice blanket — a device sort of like an air mattress filled with freezing water.

After many hours with the fever still raging, a doctor said another ice blanket would be needed.

"I was naked and I was freezing. I said, 'Doc, what could be more deluxe than this one?'" It turns out they wanted the second ice blanket to put on top of him.

Now he was covered head to foot with the ice blankets, and his head was packed in ice on three sides.

"Now I'm really cold. For three days I was afraid to fall asleep. I was afraid I'd die."

The doctor examined Hovde and frankly told him that he was likely to die. "I said, 'Doc, you can't kill a Norwegian, and you know it.'"

Again, on the ice blanket, he was pronounced dead. "There's no signal, they cover you up, and then there's a beep."

READY TO DEPLOY
Lance Corporal Pete Orput stands beside one of the helicopters ready to bring Marines to Saigon in the final days of the Vietnam War.

Photos from the personal collections of Peter Orput and Mark Ness.

THE FALL OF
SAIGON

As the war in Vietnam wound down to a frenzied and traumatic end, over 5,000 Americans and South Vietnamese were being airlifted out of the country every day. Mark Ness served as a co-pilot on a C-130 that flew the third to the last transport mission to South Vietnam, and Pete Orput served with the final group of Marines to escape Saigon when the North Vietnamese tanks rolled in on April 30, 1975.

Marine Lance Corporal Pete Orput's duty in Vietnam was short but not sweet.

Orput, part of the 2nd Battalion, 4th Marine Regiment, was flown into Saigon in the final days of the Republic of South Vietnam to lend some order to the evacuation of Americans and others from the country.

His unit's base of operations was the Defense Attache's Office near Tan Son Nhut Airfield. The DAO was headquarters for America's remaining military presence in Vietnam, and after the C-130's stopped flying, it was a major helicopter evacuation area.

"It was a phenomenally desperate scene," said Orput, an attorney who is now manager of the Criminal Division of the Minnesota Attorney General's Office. "The mobs outside were really desperate to get in. And they were all armed.

"People were throwing babies over the fence. Women were offering to be your slave for life. Everybody was howling and crying. It was a scene from hell.

"You could hear gunfire outside all day long. People were looting everything they could get their hands on. There was a sense of impending doom that was tremendous.

"I don't think there was a man in our unit who thought he was going to get out. You thought every helo was going to be the last one. It was like Custer's Last Stand."

The Marines biggest worry, Orput said, was that at some point the armed crowd would realize that they were not going be evacuated and then try to rush the Marines guarding the compound. "We were sure at some point we'd have to mix it up with them."

It was, he said, a constant battle to keep the near hysterical crowd at bay, and Marines constantly had to scale the fence and physically knock back the mob with rifle butts and fixed bayonets.

The fences had been reinforced with height extensions and concertina wire, but some of the crowd still tried to work their way in.

The evacuees waiting for flights out were a mixed lot, including American personnel, Europeans, and many South Vietnamese whose lives were in jeopardy as the North Vietnamese Army prepared to enter Saigon.

Late in the night on April 30, the compound was finally emptied of all those who had managed to

As time went by, the emphasis shifted to Vietnam, and Ness and the others flew to all the larger air bases there. "We flew into nearly every base, and it was very strange. All these huge ramps, and no airplanes. We would eat in these massive dining halls, and we would be the only ones in there."

The Air Force's job was bringing in tactical supplies and bringing out -- more and more as time when by -- American personnel and Vietnamese civilians.

"At first the civilians were very well dressed, and had big, heavy suitcases. Later, it was families and people who weren't so well off."

Even though as many as 5,000 to 7,000 were being flown out every night, not everybody got to go. "I'll always remember how the people lined the fences outside the ramp. I remember the looks on their faces. They really wanted to be on that airplane."

There was also a lot of material that was brought to the airport to be flown out, Ness said, everything from military gear to tools to stereos. Very little of it was transported, though, as the human cargo had precedence.

Ness heard of one F-5 fighter pilot who got his wife and five children into the cockpit for an evacuation.

While the civilian population was well aware of the impending takeover, Ness said that his conversations with the South Vietnamese military officials at the airport didn't reveal any panic. "When I talked to the operations people, they seemed unconcerned. They were still convinced the Americans would come to their rescue and push this all back."

The U.S. at one point was flying 60 sorties a night from Clark to Saigon, with planes leaving and departing every 15 minutes.

The South Vietnamese were also conducting their own airlift, and on one C-130 flight to Thailand, they managed to get 365 people in the cargo bay and another 32 people in the cockpit.

As the North Vietnamese pushed ever closer to the South Vietnamese capital, the perimeter around Tan Son Nhut Air Base grew smaller and smaller.

"Every night, you'd go into the intelligence briefing and the map would be on the wall. And every night the circle around the airport would get smaller.

"I remember the intelligence officer on April 28 saying, 'I can't believe you guys are going to fly in there again.' That was a great confidence builder. You always wondered, 'Is this the night when all hell breaks loose?'"

On that last flight in, Ness recalls helicopter gunboats circling around the airport perimeter to keep the communists at bay. The C-

< MARK NESS

sits at the crew entrance to a C-130 in southeast Asia in 1975.

> NOW A GENERAL

Mark Ness has risen through the ranks to become a general in the Minnesota Air Guard. He also flies for Northwest Airlines.

130 pilots used the same strategy they used in Cambodia, coming in high and then spiraling straight downward to the airfield.

"We'd come in with all our lights off and with the runway lights off. When we took off, we might turn on our landing lights for just a few seconds to see where we were going." On one return to Clark, bullet holes were found in the plane, but no damage had been caused.

Once on the ground in Saigon, any material the C-130s had brought in would be unloaded and the Vietnamese would be allowed up the loading ramp, often as many as 200 at a time. There were so many that they would have to stand up until the rear loading ramp was pulled up. "We used cargo nets instead of seat belts."

While the evacuees had been screened, "There was always that fear of sabotage," Ness said.

On that last mission, the C-130 was on the ground when a rocket hit another transport near the runway. "We were on the other end of the runway, so I couldn't see very much. I could see something was on fire. I heard the crew got out. We did our checklist as quickly as we could and got out of there."

Two more C-130s that were on the ground also took off, and that was the end of the large transport airlift.

Another reason the C-130 missions were canceled, Ness said, was because the North Vietnamese had attacked Tan Son Nhut that day with captured American fighter planes. It was North Vietnam's first and last air mission of the war.

In the end, hundreds of thousands of South Vietnamese managed to get out before and after the communist takeover on April 30.

A postscript to Ness' story came in later years when he was a pilot for North Central Airlines. "I'm sure I hauled some of those folks again to their new homes. Thousands of Vietnamese were sponsored in cities all over the Midwest."

Once in the early 1990s, Ness was piloting a flight that had a Boeing engineer on board. As they talked, it was determined that the engineers father may have been on one of the flights that Ness flew in the final days of Saigon. "He was so excited, and he wanted me to meet his father. It's amazing how things like that come full circle."

LAST DAYS OF SAIGON

The United States and North Vietnam reached a peace agreement on Jan. 27, 1973, and it was augmented by a second accord signed in June of that year. By the end of 1973, all U.S. military presence in South Vietnam was nearly removed.

The U.S. severely cut back military supplies in mid-1974, and the morale and effectiveness of the South Vietnamese (ARVN) forces took a nose dive.

In December of 1974, North Vietnam attacked Phuoc Binh, a provincial capital about 60 miles north of Saigon. The capture of this city convinced North Vietnam that it could now mount a full-scale invasion.

By April only a small perimeter remained around Saigon. Most of the ARVN forces had disappeared.

Americans intensified their airlift efforts, and thousands of American personnel and South Vietnamese civilians were ferried out in large transport planes. At one point, over 5,000 people a day were being flown out of the country.

On April 29, Tan Son Nhut Air Base was closed to the transport planes because rockets and shells were beginning to reach the airfield.

After that, only helicopter airlifts were made, and the last of those were directly into and out of the Defense Attache Office near the airfield and the American Embassy in Saigon. The Marines guarding the compounds were the last to get out.

About noon on April 30, North Vietnamese tanks rolled into Saigon unopposed and captured the city. The war had begun in 1946 when independence forces under the leadership of Ho Chi Minh began fighting with the French colonial forces.

In the end, the cost of the war was staggering. The United States lost over 58,000 dead and 300,000 wounded. South Vietnam lost about 200,000 killed and a half million wounded. North Vietnam lost about 900,000 killed and an undetermined number of wounded. Over one million North and South Vietnamese civilians were killed in the war.

ON THE ROAD TO KUWAIT

Jim Noll stopped along the road to Kuwait in 1991 to pose for a photo under the highway signs.

Photos and materials from the collection of Jim Noll.

THE HIDDEN WAR AT THE PERSIAN GULF

Jim Noll, a native of Wabasha, was a decorated veteran of the Vietnam War when he joined the Army Reserve in 1971. By 1990, he was commanding officer of the 13th Psyops Battalion, a unit dedicated to undermining the enemy's ability to make war. The unit was sent to the Persian Gulf in 1991 and played a key role in getting many Iraqis to surrender before the Allied invasion even began.

The Persian Gulf War was nearly as much a war of words as it was a war of missiles, tanks, jet fighters and M-16s.

A unit from Minnesota, the 13th Psychological Operations Battalion, played a crucial role in that war, a role that with a perspective of the intervening years looks even larger.

While Saddam Hussein was preparing for the "mother of all battles," the Minnesotans were going quietly about their business of getting Saddam's troops to desert or surrender.

By the time the U.S. and its allies took control of Kuwait, there were only about 85,000 troops remaining to fight — instead of the 400,000 Saddam had sent to control his captured nation. What happened to the rest? Some had been captured, some had been killed, but most of them had just gone home.

"We were the only battalion geared to do POW psychological warfare," Jim Noll said in a recent interview. Noll was the lieutenant colonel in charge of the 13th Psyops Battalion when it was called to active duty in December of 1990.

"By the end of the war, seven out of 10 Iraqi soldiers had deserted. In some units only 10 percent might have been left in the forward positions. In some cases, there were not enough Iraqi soldiers left to drive their vehicles."

Noll is a native of Wabasha, a graduate of Winona State College in 1967, and was a teacher in St. Cloud when he got his draft notice in 1968. "I turned in my grade cards on June 4th, and on June 5th I was in the Army."

After OCS, he joined the 101st Airborne and took part in the three and one-half month battle for Firebase Ripcord in Vietnam as a platoon leader. He was wounded twice during that action.

He earned a Silver Star and Bronze Star in addition to his Purple Hearts.

Noll got out of the Army in 1971, returned to teaching, and also joined the Army Reserve at Ft. Snelling. Along the way, over the next two decades, he was named commander of the 13th Psyops Battalion.

The Minnesotans were activated in December of 1990 and sent to Ft. Bragg where the unit had two weeks to get organized. It arrived in Saudi Arabia on the 13th of January.

Noll was the highest ranking Minnesotan to serve in the Persian Gulf War.

The battalion's job was to make the enemy quit without fighting, but how do you go about getting an enemy to go home?

For the 13th Psyops Battalion, it started in the POW camps run by the Allies. A number of Iraqis had been taken prisoner during the early skirmishes of the war. Others trickled in as time went by.

Part of the Psyops job was to get the prisoners to comply with regulations and keep the problems at a minimum. Another job was to interview the prisoners and find out ways to convince their comrades, who were still in arms, to desert or surrender.

"The MPs carried the weapons, and they were the bad guys. We were the good guys," Noll said. "The MPs greatly respected the Psyops people because we made their job so much easier."

For instance, the Psyops people would show movies every night just outside the fence. If the prisoners had not behaved that day, they saw no movie. "We had some Iraqi movies that were made according to strict Muslim laws, but they didn't want to see those. They wanted to see 'Superman.'"

Cigarettes, extra food and candy were also used to reward good behavior or cooperation. The Iraqis were provided with prayer mats and signs that indicated the direction to Mecca. "We wanted to show them that we were taking good care of them, and so they had no fear in surrendering to Americans."

The psychological specialists would interview prisoners from morning to night. Unlike American prisoners of war who are trained to keep silent, the Iraqis generally had no compunction about spilling the beans about troop placements, missile locations or other valuable war information.

They also didn't mind talking about who might be trying to escape. "We tried to identify who the Republican Guards and the secret police were. We wanted to isolate those who we felt had the potential to cause problems.

"They had no code of conduct. They would simply tell all, about underground munitions dumps, or units that hadn't been in combat yet, whatever."

From these interviews, a strategy was developed to convince the Iraqis to leave their units.

"You've got to remember that many of the Iraqi units were isolated electronically from other units. The U.S. was blocking most of the radio signals, and we were overriding Iraqi radio. In some cases we were replacing their messages with our own messages."

The U.S. would air drop little portable radios into an Iraqi unit to help get the word out. At other times, thousands of leaflets would be dropped.

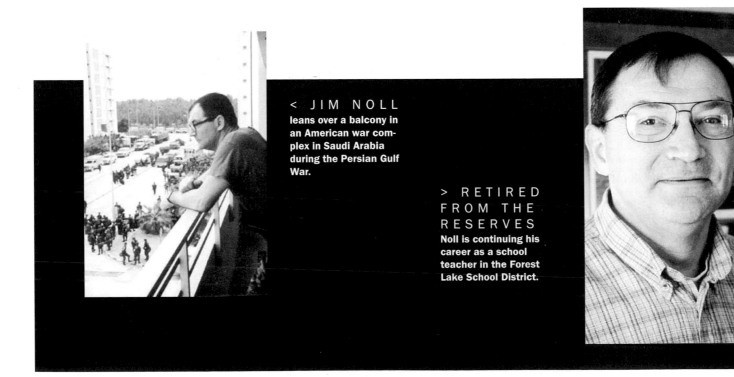

< JIM NOLL
leans over a balcony in an American war complex in Saudi Arabia during the Persian Gulf War.

> RETIRED FROM THE RESERVES
Noll is continuing his career as a school teacher in the Forest Lake School District.

One strategy was to warn the Iraqis of an impending bombing attack and then follow through. "We would tell a particular unit that we would bomb them within 24 hours and they must leave. A lot of them would do just that. We would follow through on the bombing so they knew we were telling the truth.

"The next day we would inform the next Iraqi unit in line that we would be bombing within 24 hours. We'd tell them to just leave the area and leave their equipment. A lot of them would go home. They'd just start hoofing it."

Noll noted that the Iraqis had been waiting for war for many months, and many had earned a furlough at home. "Those who had any brains never came back."

The psychological warfare in the end saved many lives, on both sides. "I know many American lives were saved because so many Iraqis had deserted or chose not to fight when we arrived. Many of them were holding up our leaflets to surrender with."

The leaflets were based on the intelligence the Psyops battalion had gained from prisoners. Some leaflets showed large bombers dropping their payloads. Others showed tank units how to surrender. Others showed Americans landing from the sea (a military ploy to divert Iraqi defenses. The U.S. never did land from the sea.) Others were printed on fake Iraqi money so the soldiers could conceal them in their wallets.

In the end, over 14 million leaflets were dropped to Iraqi troops. Some were even delivered in bottles that washed up on shore.

The pictures were important. "Many Iraqis only had enough education to read the Koran, and that was it."

Once a leaflet was developed, it was tried with the prisoners to find out how effective it might be. In one case, a leaflet went out with a red border. The Iraqi troops had been instructed that red meant danger, and the leaflets were not used. After switching to a green border, the results improved dramatically.

Noll had Saudi and Kuwaiti soldiers who were bilingual assigned to his unit that helped with the testing of the materials by working with the prisoners of war.

The Iraqis also tried some crude psychological warfare of their own. One particular leaflet told an American soldier that Bart Simpson was at home with his wife. Apparently the Iraqis didn't realize that Bart was a cartoon character.

Only once in the POW camps was there a major problem. A typhoon hit one of the camps one night, and the guards,

A PORTRAIT OF SADDAM
was one of the items liberated by Noll during the liberation of Kuwait in the Persian Gulf War. The photo was hung in an office building.

who were not U.S. soldiers, deserted their posts. Psyops soldiers with speaker backpacks went into the camp where chaos reigned, and with the help of local officials restored order.

In addition to the Psyops units working in the camps, each American unit had three psyops specialists assigned to it. The job of these tactical units was to make contact with the enemy and encourage them to surrender.

The strategy was especially important because when the U.S. did attack, the armored units raced across the desert to confront Iraqi tank units. In the process, many Iraqi army units were simply bypassed. It was important to convince those bypassed units to surrender rather than fight.

When Kuwait had been retaken by the Allies, Noll entered the city the next day. He urged the command to release his tactical units, spread out throughout the American forces, so they could be used to help control the huge influx of enemy prisoners.

The Americans also trained the Saudis in the aspects of psychological warfare and dealing with prisoners because the prisoners were soon turned over to the Saudi army for safekeeping.

The 13th Psyops Battalion left in May, and turned over all the POW camps to the Saudis.

"My unit may have saved thousands of lives during the war, on both sides."

Noll returned to his home south of Forest Lake just in time for his daughter's first communion. In the next year, he volunteered for the U.S. Army War College in Pennsylvania, and he returned to command the 88th Regular Supply Command. His last job in the Reserves was as director of personnel for a six-state area, including about 25,000 soldiers.

He retired in June 1999 as a colonel.

Noll is a teacher at Forest Lake Southwest Junior High School. He and his wife, Rose, have eight children.

THE IRAQIS ALSO TRIED

to propagandize the Allies during the war. A leaflet below compares the Persian Gulf War to the Vietnam War.

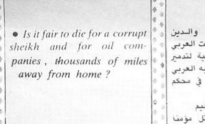

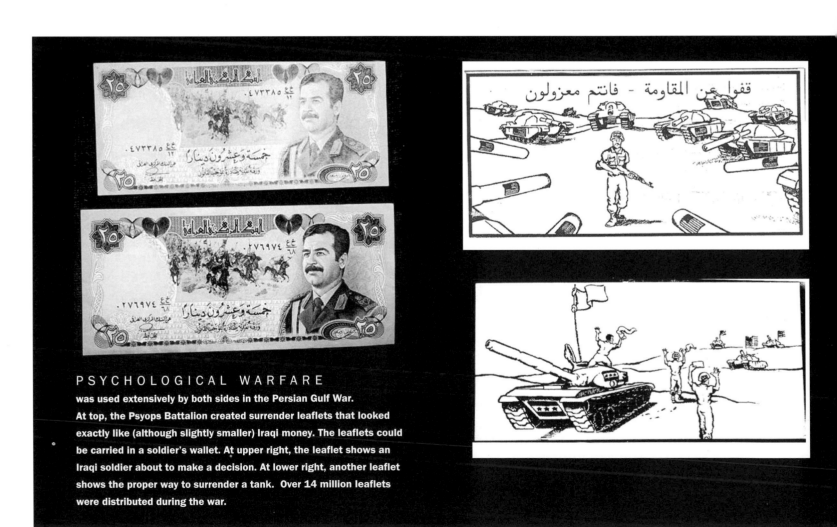

PSYCHOLOGICAL WARFARE

was used extensively by both sides in the Persian Gulf War. At top, the Psyops Battalion created surrender leaflets that looked exactly like (although slightly smaller) Iraqi money. The leaflets could be carried in a soldier's wallet. At upper right, the leaflet shows an Iraqi soldier about to make a decision. At lower right, another leaflet shows the proper way to surrender a tank. Over 14 million leaflets were distributed during the war.

Al Zdon

is a writer and editor who was born and raised in Minneapolis. A graduate of the University of Minnesota School of Journalism, he was the managing editor of the *Hibbing Daily Tribune* for nearly 20 years. He is presently the editor of the *Minnesota Legionnaire*.

He and his wife, Mary, have six children: Anna, Corinna, Zachary, Larissa, Nathaniel, and Delaney.

Zdon is a member of the School of Journalism's Alumni Board, and he is a member in good standing of the Greater Mesabi Men's Book Club. He enjoys basketball and tennis and playing the tenor banjo. He is currently enrolled in the Masters of Liberal Studies Program at the University of Minnesota.

He is the owner of Moonlit Eagle Productions, a writing and publishing company. Zdon is a Navy veteran of the Vietnam War.